THE RED MOVEMENT

# THE
# RED MOVEMENT:

*Social and Environmental Justice in the 21st Century*

BY

SHADAN KAPRI

◊ KP ◊

KAPRI PUBLISHING

Join us in our global mission to change the world with education and books.

For more information visit KapriPublishing.com

ISBN: 978-1-7346446-4-7 (paperback) / 978-1-7346446-5-4 (eBook)

The author has made every possible effort to provide accurate internet addresses at the time of publication. Neither the author nor the publisher assumes responsibility for errors or changes to internet addresses after date of publication since the publisher has no control over third-party websites.

This book is dedicated to my Mother,
who taught me the most important lesson in life:
the best way to find yourself
is to lose yourself in the service of humanity.
I love you eternally, Mom.
This book is written for you.
May all your sacrifices be finally worth it.

It is also written
for anyone out there who has ever wondered
if their life was meant for something *greater*.
You were born to make a difference
in small ways, in large ways, in every way.
May this book help you in realizing one powerful truth:
this world needs *you*.

# TABLE OF CONTENTS

## Why is it called THE RED MOVEMENT?

Red symbolizes blood. It symbolizes life.

Regardless of our differences, we all have red blood running through our body.

It's the color that binds us as human beings.

It's a color that reminds us of our shared humanity.

After all, injustice anywhere is injustice everywhere.

And it's up to us, collectively, as Mothers, Fathers, Sisters, Brothers, Children, Friends, Neighbors, and Co-Workers to stop social injustices before another generation is victimized.

The fight will take all of us.

We each have an important role to play.

And the purpose of this movement is to help people understand their role, and unite them together in the fight against social injustice.

**That is why it's called THE RED MOVEMENT.**

**Social Justice** is the fair and equal treatment of all people in a society regardless of race, gender, sexual orientation, or background and the equitable distribution of resources and benefits to all members of a community. The cornerstones of social justice are racial equality, personal and public accountability, and preserving human rights and dignity.

**Environmental Justice** is the right to live, work, and play in a healthy, safe, and clean environment without life threatening conditions or threats. It promotes environmental, economic, and social justice by revealing the link between the communities people live in and equal rights and protections under the law.

**Human trafficking is a form of modern-day slavery** that involves the recruitment, transportation, or transfer of a person by improper and illegal methods such as deception, coercion, force, fraud, threats, violence, or abduction for sexual exploitation or forced labor.

## Two Main Types of Human Trafficking

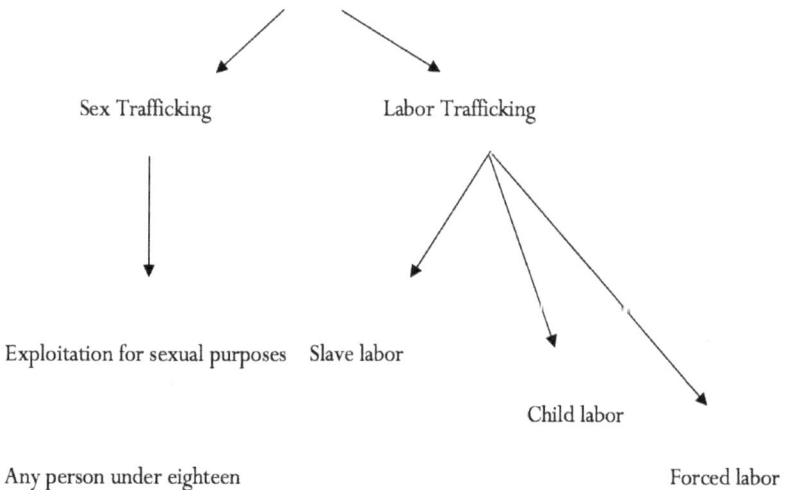

Sex Trafficking

Labor Trafficking

Exploitation for sexual purposes

Slave labor

Child labor

Any person under eighteen

who is lured into prostitution

is defined as a victim of sex

trafficking under state and

federal laws in the United States.

Forced labor

# INTRODUCTION

The world watched in horror as George Floyd's life came down to its very last moments. "Please, I can't breathe," he repeated 27 times in less than five minutes. No one at the time knew it, but his death and its subsequent video would ignite a new wave of civil rights protest and action the world had not seen for decades.

Those final minutes of George Floyd's life shocked some Americans who lived in denial about racism, discrimination, and social injustice today. While for others the video was a glimpse into the undercurrent of race-relations and violence they endure on a daily basis.

Less than a year later the murder trial over George Floyd's death began and some were concerned at what a potential not-guilty verdict could mean for America. Was the trial going to be another example of a broken legal system with an implicit bias or would it foster accountability and transparency in a world still reeling by the pain of three unforgettable words, "I can't breathe."

Three weeks later the nation prepared for the verdict. Camera crews descended onto the Minneapolis courthouse.

When the guilty verdicts were finally read an eruption of cheers and relief spread throughout the crowd.

Was this verdict a new chapter in fighting social injustice and creating accountability in America or just a temporary pause on greater problems that have been continuously ignored? No one knows for sure but everyone can agree that it had been a brutal year for America. Covid-19 ran rapid killing millions of people. Yet even with a global pandemic thousands of American citizens had left their homes and potentially risked their lives to protest the use of excessive force by police officers against minorities.

Every time a new name was added to the list of victims of police brutality, the nation braced for a potential new wave of unrest. Now that the trial of the century was over some began to see the possibility for a new resurgence. Was Black Lives Matter and the murder of George Floyd ushering in a new civil rights movement in America? Was this a step at finally confronting the use of excessive force by white officers and stopping the mass incarceration of black people? In other words, would we move forward as a nation under peace or continue to become divided by race?

What many people didn't know was behind the scenes a new movement was forming. A movement that took Black Lives Matter to the next level by showing how the racist ideology and patterns were part of much wider global problem embedded into almost every aspect of modern-day life.

This new movement would be called The Red Movement. And it would help people understand their important role in the fight for social justice in the midst of the Black Lives Matter Movement and the George Floyd tragedy. The events of the last year forced a reckoning of where America is as a nation and the role that each of us plays moving forward.

In many ways, we are in the middle of the greatest human rights and environmental crises in history. *The Black Lives Matter Movement is the tip of the iceberg when it comes to confronting, understanding, and dismantling systemic racism, discrimination, and social injustice in America and around the world today.*

Optimists hoped that these events would open the door to an even deeper understanding of social injustices in the 21st Century. While pessimistic were convinced that America would fail to confront its racist ideology that led to this crisis once again. Would America live up to its ideals and become united once again? Or would race relations divide us as a country as we fail to take this opportunity to foster real change?

Racism, discrimination, and social injustices never went away. Black Lives Matter and the George Floyd tragedy reintroduced it to Americans who lived in denial about its expansion. As much as these current events pushed social awareness forward, they are just the beginning to understanding the world we live in today.

Systemic racism and discrimination are rooted in slavery. Some even describe them as a by-product or symptoms of slavery which begs the question, "How can the symptoms (racism and discrimination) be eradicated when the root cause (slavery) has only gotten worse?"

The system of historic oppression inherent in slavery never went away. It just transitioned into something more prevalent and embedded in our lives than ever before. And each of us unknowingly bought into it literally and figuratively.

While the world is declared 'slave free,' the truth is just the opposite. People are still bought and sold in public auctions, forced to sell their bodies for sex, or work in hidden factories or farms under unbearable conditions. Some even toil away on construction sites for the world's most famous sporting events.

Just like systemic racism and discrimination, slavery never really ended. It just changed form, and Black Lives Matter showed a glimpse into a much deeper and wider global problem plaguing the world today thereby becoming the precursor to The Red Movement.

The Red Movement is a grassroots international movement that helps people understand their role in the fight for social and environmental justice in the midst of the Black Lives Matter Movement and the George Floyd murder.

People have enormous power as a group and individuals to make a difference. We've seen this happen in history time and time again from America's Independence to the Civil War and the Civil Rights Movement of the 1950's and 60's. People have come together to make an impact that transcends their generation, an impact that transcends their time by working together to create a new future, a new consciousness, a global shift that leaves behind rippling effects for generations to come. These changes are a testament to the values held close to people's hearts. Legacies that far outlive any one person or any one time.

*This time is absolutely no different.*

The Black Lives Matter Movement and global protests began to tap into that power. It helped people understand how they can't wait on governments or non-profits to end these problems otherwise we wouldn't be dealing with them today.

*The average everyday person has enormous power to right these wrongs in ways that few realize, until now. Until the Red Movement.*

The Red Movement ushers in a new era by helping people understand how some of the worst modern-day injustices, racism, and discrimination have been supported and expanded by unchecked consumerism.

Think of it this way, if one person buys a product from a company or supports an event that results in the violation of basic human rights or environmental degradation nothing happens. Yet, when millions of people buy products from the same company or support the same event that exploits people and the planet then *we are collectively promoting and expanding these social injustices every day.*

People have inadvertently supported social injustice, racism, discrimination, and the source of these problems - modern-day slavery - by purchasing products and supporting corporations who use slave or forced labor, exploit their workers basic human rights, expose them to dangerous conditions, deny them a livable wage, dump toxic chemicals and materials into the environment, or overflow landfills with hazardous waste and toxins.

By buying these products and thereby supporting these companies we engage in unchecked consumerism that is ravaging our planet and leading to the greatest human rights and environmental crises in history.

The Black Lives Matter Movement opened people's eyes to the injustices happening in plain sight. The Red Movement pushes that door wide open to the injustices *we don't see but can be just as harmful.* The mission of The Red Movement is to empower people to make conscious choices that align with their beliefs by supporting corporations, practices, companies, events, and even policies that **promote and foster human rights and environmental protections for generations to come.**

Consumerism and business must be used as a force for good and many young consumers are demanding this change in the era of Black Lives Matter. A business model that exploits people and the Earth is no longer sustainable or acceptable in the name of "profit." These are the principles the Red Movement is built upon.

The first step of The Red Movement is to raise awareness. Few realize it, but items made or harvested by the labor of modern-day slaves are so embedded in our daily lives that we are literally surrounded by them from certain foods we eat to clothes we wear to coffee and chocolate harvested by child slaves. Slave labor is even used in mining and those basic raw materials too often find their way into electronics, computers, smartphones, cars, cosmetics and even jewelry.

The Red Movement pushes the issue of social justice forward by creating a global grassroots effort to stop systemic discrimination, racism, and modern-day slavery through awareness, advocacy, and action.

Protests are a great start, but they are only the start.

Current approaches to addressing systemic racism and discrimination have failed partly because they have addressed the symptoms and not the root causes of these problems: modern-day slavery. That is main question facing the nation now, "Who will we become moving forward, part of the problem or part of the solution?" Real change requires a new perspective, a new way of fighting these old problems because what we've have been doing so far is not working.

Ultimately, how can we support and advocate for Black Lives Matter and then turn around and buy products made by slave labor or forced labor and call that progress? We can't and that is why the Red Movement is vital in the next chapter to fighting social and environmental injustice in America and around the world today.

# PART I:

# INVISIBLE LIVES

# CHAPTER ONE

# THE HIDDEN SIDE
# OF CHOCOLATE

*The Black Lives Matter Movement exposed some of the injustices in
plain sight.
Yet what about the injustices we don't see?
The injustices that are hidden.
What is our role in fighting those problems?
In other words, is Black Lives Matter just the beginning?*

In 2000, a series of newspaper articles exposed the shocking
connection between child slavery and the chocolate industry.[1] Before that year few people outside of Africa even knew of
the problem. Then a turning point in 2000 thrust the chocolate
industry into the blinding international spotlight—a spotlight
they have shunned ever since.

The newspaper articles revealed that behind the innocent
images of chocolate existed a much darker side, a side companies strongly denied while journalists, activists, and scholars wrote countless reports, articles, and books revealing a
very unsettling reality regarding the child slaves of chocolate. Investigative documentaries followed showing children

smuggled from neighboring countries to the cocoa farms of the Ivory Coast.[2]

According to the book *The Dark Side of Chocolate*, hundreds of thousands of black children, some as young as seven, were trafficked to harvest cocoa beans in the Ivory Coast every year.[3] This was a startling discovery because the Ivory Coast is home to *over 70 percent of the world's cocoa supply.*[4] Cocoa beans are the main ingredient in chocolate meaning most of the world's chocolate comes from the Ivory Coast.

For years the lives of these hidden "slaves of chocolate" were shrouded in an air of secrecy while they were paid miniscule wages, denied the basic right to an education, abused, neglected, coerced, and in certain cases used as slave labor.[5]

The investigative book *Chocolate Nations: Living and Dying for Cocoa in West Africa*, written by Orla Ryan, revealed even more to the mysterious and dangerous side of harvesting chocolate's main ingredient cocoa beans.[6]

> Traffickers preyed on children at bus stops in Mali, promising riches on cocoa farms in Cote d'Ivoire. Once children got to the farm, they survived on little food, little or no pay and endured regular beatings. There were no chains and no irons, but unable to leave their place of work, they were effectively slaves, harvesting the beans that were the key ingredient for chocolate.[7]

The harsh reality baffled many because the chocolate industry made millions in profit every year.[8] Yet the accusations of child trafficking and slavery began haunting their once golden reputation.

Initially the chocolate industry denied the claims. Then, in 2001, the largest chocolate manufacturers signed an agreement prohibiting child labor and trafficking in the cocoa industry after 2008.[9] This agreement was called the Harkin-Engel Protocol, named after the men who championed the cause, U.S. Representative Eliot Engel and Senator Tom Harkin.[10] They initially introduced a law requiring a labeling system for the chocolate industry that revealed whether the sweets were *slave-free or not.*[11]

The chocolate giants fought back on the labeling system, and the international compromise became known as the Harkin-Engel Protocol (or the Cocoa Protocol.) The goal was to end the worst forms of child labor in the production of cocoa. This agreement outlined how chocolate companies would "wean" themselves off of child labor and show certification (proof).

Yet this would not require labeling products as "slave-free" as the initial legislation had proposed instead it would require "public reporting by African governments, third-party verification and poverty remediation."[12]

Deadlines were given, and the initial deadline of 2005 passed without the Protocol being met. The deadline was extended to 2008 and then again to 2018.[13] Progress was being made, but some wondered whether the extension to 2020 would finally be the year the Protocol was completely satisfied.

The goal of the 2020 extension was to reduce child labor in the cocoa industry by 70 percent. According to the Cocoa Barometer 2018 report, "Not a single company or government is anywhere near reaching the sector wide objective of the elimination of child labor, and not even near their commitment of a 70% reduction of child labor by 2020."[14] Does this mean that every cocoa farm perpetuates slavery in Africa? No, absolutely not. But enough of them are tainted by slavery that it makes it a serious concern for the U.S. government and the United Nations.

To monitor the progress in reaching the Harkin-Engel Protocol's modest goals, the U.S. government began working with Tulane University in New Orleans. After considerable research and investigations, Tulane published a report in 2009.[15] The report shocked some outside the chocolate industry. It painted a haunting picture of the slaves of chocolate. The researchers estimated that over *eight hundred thousand children* in Cote d'Ivoire and *almost one million* in Ghana had worked on cocoa farms in the last year before their report was published.[16]

Within both countries, more than half a million black children worked in conditions that violated international labor guidelines and national laws on hours and ages. More than half the children reported an injury. "About 5 percent of children in Côte d'Ivoire and 10 percent in Ghana worked for pay."[17] Did this constitute slavery or simply the working conditions in the third world? Experts disagree, but one aspect has consensus across the board: change has been incredibly slow.

Even though the past two decades brought intense attention to the child slaves of chocolate, the problem still persists today, and the deadline for satisfying the protocol completely have been continuously pushed back.

Yet millions of consumers remain unaware of the scandal in the chocolate industry and how their simple buying power is impacting thousands of lives. To combat the inequality, Fair

Trade chocolate has gained momentum as stories have trickled out of the Ivory Coast.

Fair Trade is a movement to help producers in third world countries get a fair price for their products with the goal of decreasing poverty, providing fair treatment for farmers and workers, and promoting practices that are environmentally sustainable. Farmers in the Ivory Coast should be paid not just a fair price but a living wage to sustain their farms and have the money to pay their workers.

Some within the chocolate industry have made attempts to improve the problem by joining the International Cocoa Initiative.[18] The initiative is a partnership that brings together the giants of chocolate, nonprofit organizations, labor unions, and cocoa processors.[19]

Some of the biggest names in chocolate have joined the initiative in a good faith attempt to deal with the problem. However, the most important questions remain unanswered: Have these actions brought the industry any closer to achieving the very modest goals of the Harkin-Engel Protocol? If not, then what needs to be done? When will it finally be reached and how can the chocolate industry become free of child slaves, child labor, and trafficking?

In other words, what will it really take to make chocolate a slave-free product?

Lawsuits?

A series of public relations nightmares?

Dead children?

Sadly, the answer is all of the above.

## THE LAWSUITS BEGIN

In July 2005, three unnamed former child slaves from Mali filed a class action lawsuit against chocolate giants Nestlé, Cargill, and Archer Daniels Midland in California.[20] This lawsuit was groundbreaking. A quintessential example of David versus Goliath. The striking difference was that David (in this case the former child slaves) needed to remain anonymous. Global Exchange, a human rights organization, joined as Plaintiffs with the three unnamed child slaves.

Nestlé, not one for backing down, filed a motion to force disclosure of the names of the three former child slaves, named merely as John Doe I, John Doe II, and John Doe III in the lawsuit.[21] The child slaves opposed the motion for safety reasons, not only for themselves but their family members who still lived in the unstable area of the Ivory Coast. In addition to forcing disclosure of the Plaintiffs' names, the chocolate giants also requested a motion to dismiss the case entirely.[22] They wanted this to go away as quickly as possible.

It seemed as if Goliath and his army of attorneys were winning when the court ordered a dismissal of the case for failure to state a claim upon which relief could be granted.[23] The case was gone, but what would happen next? Would the case even make a dent in the larger global problem of black child slavery?

At the time no one knew it, but the war was just beginning. The reversal was appealed, and as news of the case grew, attorneys from around the nation offered to help by writing amicus briefs (at no charge) and providing legal assistance in support of reversing the dismissal and giving it new life.

Legal scholars from Harvard Law School and Northwestern University, along with others from around the nation, became interested, and the list of attorneys helping to reverse the dismissal became a "Who's Who" of experts in legal history, international law, and international human rights.

David finally had a fighting chance in conquering Goliath.

All the hard work paid off. The dismissal of the case was reversed by the Ninth Circuit. The battle was given a new chance to continue. In the judicial opinion written by Senior Circuit Judge Dorothy Wright Nelson, the court summarized how the Plaintiffs were forced to work up to fourteen hours a day with only scraps of food to sustain their lives.[24] They were "whipped and beaten" and "locked in small rooms at night and not permitted to leave the plantations, knowing that the children who tried to escape would be beaten or tortured. Plaintiff John Doe II witnessed guards cut open the feet of children who attempted to escape, and John Doe II knew that the guards forced failed escapees to drink urine."[25]

The legal opinion went on to describe how the Defendants in the case (Nestlé, Cargill, and Archer Daniels Midland) dominated the Ivory Coast cocoa market, since their work is "largely in charge of...buying and selling cocoa" and importing "most of the Ivory Coast's cocoa harvest into the United States."[26]

Yet the most damaging part of the opinion was just beginning:

> The defendants are well aware of the child slavery problem in the Ivory Coast. They acquired this knowledge firsthand through their numerous visits to Ivorian farms. Additionally, the defendants knew of the child slave labor problems

> in the Ivorian cocoa sector due to the many
> reports issued by domestic and international
> organizations.

> Despite their knowledge of child slavery and
> their control over the cocoa market, the de-
> fendants operate in the Ivory Coast 'with the
> unilateral goal of finding the cheapest sources
> of cocoa.'[27]

If those sentences in the legal opinion were not the smok-
ing gun human rights advocates were hoping for, then nothing
would be. It showed that these companies knew about child
slavery yet still *looked for the cheapest cocoa to buy.* This scathing
order against the Plaintiffs went on to reverse the dismissal of
the case and allowed the child slaves to change their complaint
and refile their lawsuit.

"The court found that the Plaintiffs have standing to bring
their Alien Tort case because of the universal prohibition against
slavery."[28] Essentially, the corporate entities were not immune
from their actions based on their corporate status. The battle
between David and Goliath was given another round.

The chocolate giants, not wanting to lose while having millions of dollars at their disposal, petitioned the U.S. Supreme
Court to throw out the lower court's ruling regarding the
appeal.[29] The U.S. Supreme Court declined to hear the case
in January 2016, and the lower court's ruling remained the
final decision in the appeal.[30]

This was a huge victory for the former child slaves and the
army of legal scholars who had come to their defense, since it

meant that for the first-time corporations could be held legally accountable in the United States for their actions in supporting slavery abroad, either directly or indirectly through financial assistance. There was no complete immunity to shield or protect their actions according to the Ninth Circuit's ruling. This was a win not only for the Plaintiffs but potentially for every child slave around the world whose products would be sold overseas.

Was slavery really dead, as millions of people believed? No, not even close. It had transitioned to a new system of oppression that was hidden and more prevalent, but this legal victory would turn the page in an international problem that was starting to finally come to light. David finally had a real chance. This case increased the glaring spotlight on the chocolate industry and created momentum never seen before.

In July 2016, the Plaintiffs amended their complaint. The chocolate giants again requested for the case to be dismissed, and a judge dismissed the case because the court found the wrongdoing overseas was not linked to U.S. companies.

The child slaves and their allies filed another appeal on the basis that Nestle's and Cargill's decision to give cocoa farmers financial and technical support happened at their U.S. Headquarters thereby linking the case to the United States.

The Ninth Circuit of the Court of Appeals sided with the child slaves again and allowed the case to continue against Nestle and Cargill under the Alien Tort Statute because of the universal prohibition against slavery.

Ultimately, would this case continue and help other cases? Could others come forward and file similar lawsuits? Those questions are unknown at this time since litigation is still pending. Yet it can be argued that justice is closer for child slaves because of this one case that has bounced between U.S. courts for the last fifteen years.

Another class action lawsuit was also filed in September of 2015 against three of the country's largest chocolate companies—Mars, Nestlé, and Hershey—by consumers in a California federal court. "Plaintiffs Robert Hodson, Elaine McCoy, and Laura Dana respectively filed the [Mars, Nestlé, and Hershey] class action lawsuit[s]."[31]

In Robert Hodson's lawsuit against Mars, he claimed that had he known of the problems and links between modern-day slavery and the company's award-winning chocolate bars, he would have never bought them.[32]

All three alleged the same points—the companies should not ignore the human rights abuses linked to the industry, and failure to disclose the use of slave labor in their supply chains meant that consumers were deceived into buying products and supporting slavery through their purchases.[33] They asserted that the public had the right to know of these abuses through honest labeling of products. The consumers also claimed that the chocolate giants violated the California Unfair Competition Law, the False Advertising Law, and the Consumer Legal Remedies Act.[34]

A leading civil rights consumer law firm, Hagens Berman, filed all three lawsuits on behalf of the consumers. Nestlé responded with an official statement that child labor had no place in Nestlé's business model and future. Nestlé also stated that they were taking steps to eliminate child labor by tackling the root cause.[35] However, specific examples were not provided.

Mars responded in a statement by stating that child labor is a "serious and complex" problem and they are committed to the solution.[36] In 2009, Mars had pledged to be child- and slave-free by 2020 (not accomplished to date). And finally, Hershey's response was that the "allegations in the lawsuit [are] not new and reflect long-term challenges" in the industry. [37] They cited their involvement in attempting to have a clean supply chain by 2020.[38]

Yet the case took a dramatic turn when all three lawsuits were dismissed in the beginning of 2016 to the surprise of many. U.S. Magistrate Judge Joseph C. Spero and U.S. District Judge Richard Seeborg dismissed the cases because the law (as it currently stands) does not require the chocolate giants to disclose "child or slave labor" on their products.[39]

The dismissal was a blow for human rights activists and consumers, but it made it painfully clear that the **laws in California and around the nation needed to be changed in order to force companies to disclose whether child or slave labor are a part of their supply chain**. There had been an attempt to pass such a law years before, but lobbying by the chocolate giants had stopped the efforts and turned the crusade from a binding law into a "voluntary agreement" between the chocolate companies to attempt to become slave free.

Had the legislature dropped the ball? Could California have passed its own laws requiring the truth in disclosing slave and child labor in food products? Had the federal judges missed an opportunity to use the legal system as a real tool for social justice reform? The answer to all of these is a profound yes, but this was just one battle against modern-day injustice, discrimination, and racism. The war, in many ways, was only beginning.

Each person comes into this world for a specific purpose.
A specific destiny.
A message to share.
Actions to fulfill.
No one is here by accident.
There is an important reason for your existence.

CHAPTER TWO

# WHAT IS THE RED MOVEMENT?

I n 2006, a former Vatican Envoy to the United Nations ex-posed a shocking secret.[40] Slavery is more widespread now than ever before in history.[41] Although shrouded in mystery, the secret lives of people living in slave-like conditions today have profound meaning. Their daily struggles expose the dark truth that modern-day slavery, injustice, racism, and discrimi-nation not only exist but are flourishing in parts of the world today.

During the transatlantic slave trade, more than 12 million people were sold into slavery (for sexual and labor purposes). The number of people living in slave-like conditions today is more than three times that amount at over 40 million.[42] It's a secret more profitable than Starbucks, Google, and Amazon combined.[43]

*The reality is that modern-day slavery, racism, and discrimina-tion are all around us.* They have infiltrated various areas of our lives since modern-day slavery can be traced back to almost every industry from food to fashion, diamonds to toys, coffee, chocolate, computers, smartphones and even large-scale sporting events like the Super Bowl and World Cup. The products from modern-day slavery are so entrenched in our daily lives that we are literally surrounded by them yet fail to see their prevalence in almost every aspect of our lives.

## THE WORLD OF LABOR TRAFFICKING

While sex trafficking has exploded in the last twenty years, so has its counterpart labor trafficking. Some of the most common items in any home are likely made, harvested, or put together by slave labor, child labor, or forced labor.[44]

You may be wondering, "How is this possible, when slavery was abolished over a century ago? More importantly, what can we do end this?"

Welcome to the Red Movement. We've been waiting for you. The purpose of this book is to light a match that ignites the Red Movement around the world and inspires a new wave of social justice reform from the ground up.

The Red Movement is a global call to action, of people from all backgrounds and faiths to stop racism, discrimination, modern-day slavery, social injustice, and environmental destruction by raising awareness of how our daily innocent purchases, decisions, and unchecked consumerism have unintentionally pushed these problems forward at an unthinkable rate without our consent or knowledge. We've all contributed to creating this problem, now we all need to fight against it.

Look at it this way, if one person buys a product or supports an event that results in the abuse of human rights or environmental depletion, nothing happens, *but when millions of people*

*buy a product from the same company or support the same event, then*
*we are supporting and growing the very injustices that we are against.*

Every day millions of people unknowingly purchase products created, put together, or harvested by slave or forced labor thereby supporting corporations who *mistreat their workers, violate their basic human rights, expose them to dangerous environments, deny them a livable wage. At the same time some of these corporations are dumping toxic chemicals and materials into the environment, or overflowing landfills with hazardous wastes and materials.*

We unknowingly support slavery, social injustice, and the degradation of the environment with every poor buying choice we make. In a sense, we become innocent, unknowing co-conspirators to a global injustice that circles the Earth and has grown at an unprecedented rate. All because we have been asleep at the wheel.

The purpose of the Red Movement is to uncover those secrets and empower people to act in ways that promote human rights and environmental protections. The Red Movement inspires and educates people towards change for themselves and future generations to come.

Once we face the truth about modern-day social injustices and how connected they are to our daily lives, that is the moment everything can change. That is the moment the tides can turn. Nothing in life can be fixed unless the truth is faced straight on, and some people spend their entire lives running away from the truth and running away from their own power to change it. Until now.

The purpose of the Red Movement is not to cast blame but grow and support companies, and events that are *doing good in this world.* It's about educating ourselves on the impact of our spending and voting with our dollar in every aspect of our lives.

While some corporations and big businesses may not mind if the connection between human trafficking, modern-day injustices, racism, and common everyday products remain a mystery, others are working hard to create corporate cultures and missions that embody the spirit of preserving human rights by dealing with this head-on. These companies understand that by selling products that use slave labor, forced labor, or child labor, they not only contribute to the problem but push its expansion forward.

This movement strives to promote conscious consumerism that supports products, corporations, practices, and even large-scale events that leave behind a positive legacy for ourselves, our children, and the Earth.

If anything, people from all generations have one thing in common. They want to be a part of something greater than themselves. They want to be a part of a group that leaves behind an unforgettable mark. They want to make an impact. If there is any sense of "entitlement," it is born out of the belief that rules and fairness should apply to everyone and not escape a select few.

Corporations, multinational companies, and the wealthy must adhere to the same standards the rest of us live by. No one gets a free pass because of wealth or privilege. These are the principles the Red Movement is built upon.

The goals of the Red Movement are to create a global conscious shift that sends a clear message. We, as human beings, are aware of where our hard-earned money is going, and we will not support products, practices, events, or companies that contribute to the violation of basic human rights or the destruction of our environment.

Not now.

Not ever.

The Red Movement begins now.

The most important question is, "Will you join us?"

If not, "Then who will, and what will it finally take?"

"Passionate and well-articulated ideas
can and do change the world.
Long after buildings and aqueducts have crumbled,
writers' words live on."

—Mary Pipher

CHAPTER THREE

# IT IS EVERYWHERE

I t's no secret that chocolate and coffee are some of the most sought-after items for consumers today. For millions of people, their daily mocha or frappuccino helps them function in a fast-paced world. Coffee is so valuable that Americans spend on average $4 billion each year just bringing coffee into the country.

Every single day, over one hundred million people drink their magic coffee concoction spending more than $200 million *each day* on their daily fix. Surely, given the staggering profits, slavery and social injustice are not a part of the coffee industry as well, right?

Unfortunately, that's a secret some coffee insiders don't want you to know. Coffee is one of the industries tainted by slave labor and child labor.[45] If you buy your coffee at a café, 99 percent of your purchase goes to everyone but the coffee workers who actually harvested the coffee beans.[46] The majority of the staggering profits go to corporations, stores, and cafés. Too often the farmers and workers who are the backbone of the industry are categorically excluded from the millions of dollars the coffee industry profits from every single day.

Consumers are paying more than their fair share for their coffee fix, so why isn't the money trickling down to the farmers and workers that need it the most? Why is the trickle-down theory failing so miserably, to the point that slavery is even part of the conversation? The answer is simple. The coffee industry is largely unregulated, and the coffee giants often pay very little for the coffee beans that lead to our daily coffee obsession.[47] Is this fair? No, it never has been and never will be until consumers take a stand.

According to researchers at Oxfam America, when "you buy your daily cappuccino, the farmer who grew the coffee beans receives less than one percent of what you pay for it. About 6 percent of the price you pay for coffee in the supermarket goes to the farmer."[48]

Even if the coffee is not harvested by slave labor or child labor, it can still be reasonably argued (based on pure mathematics alone) that the coffee industry's economics are exploitative to the farmers and workers, who are the foundation of the industry, to the point of crippling poverty in some cases. In Guatemala, earning three dollars a day often means picking one hundred pounds of coffee beans.

Yet the answer, surprisingly, includes three simple words: Fair Trade coffee. It's not a trend but a way to ensure that farmers are paid a fair wage so their workers are also given the same basic opportunities. Some see Fair Trade coffee as the newest stylish way to become socially conscious, but in reality, if the coffee industry is to fall in line with their human rights responsibilities, Fair Trade needs to take over the industry, and it can't happen fast enough.

Yet, coffee and chocolate are only a few of the industries tainted by modern-day slavery. The largest misconception about racism, discrimination, and modern-day injustice is that it exists "out there" when in reality it exists right in our homes, right under our noses, and we are blind to it.

For example, when you go through your cupboards, closets, and rooms, have you ever stepped back for a moment and thought about the people behind the "things" you buy? Who are the people behind the products you use every day? From the trendy clothes you wear to the foods you eat and the electronics you use, even the toys you buy for your children, our lives are surrounded by their contribution to our world, *yet how much do we know about them*? And ultimately are we too afraid to ask?

Think of it this way, when you pay less for a T-shirt, or any item for that matter, are you really getting a good deal? Who pays the ultimate price for our "bargain deals" and "comfortable" lifestyles? Would we rather not know? Is ignorance bliss?

The hidden truth is that the products of *modern-day slavery, racism, discrimination, and injustice are all around us*. Today and every day, chances are you have worn, touched, or even used something made by slave labor, child labor, or forced labor. The most well-kept secret is that too many of the products we rely on—from certain coffee to clothes, apples to sugar, chocolate, toys, computers, and even cell phones—arrive to stores through a supply chain too often tainted by slave labor, child labor, or forced labor.

The Black Lives Matter Movement opened people's eyes to the injustices in plain sight. The Red Movement pushes the door wide open to the injustices we don't see but can be just as systemic and damaging. The problem is that a number of items we use every day are harvested and produced by humans who are given few chances in life.[49] These raw materials harvested by child labor, forced labor, and/or slave labor end up in the hands of multinational corporations that pay pennies on the dollar and use the materials to make products that you and I use every day. Sometimes the raw materials are exported directly to us, and other times they end up in a supply chain tainted by slavery and we are sold the creations.

This dirty secret makes some multinational corporations unbelievably rich while lives are exploited and mistreated in the name of profits. And we are the biggest consumers of these items. The crisis is real. And it impacts every aspect of our lives, so much so that the Department of Labor releases a report every year investigating and uncovering the worst forms of child labor and forced labor.[50] It's designed to be a wake-up call to the public, but the mainstream media has largely ignored this report year after year.

Even though the mainstream media has failed to talk about this report, its purpose and intent have remained clear from day one. To fight the growing crisis of modern-day slavery, social injustice, racism, and discrimination the public must be aware of the products and countries that systematically exploit people for profit and how those products end up in our hands thereby reinforcing this oppressive cycle. By buying these products we unknowingly help these companies grow and exploit a new generation of victims.

## The Hidden Truth

The real revolution is the evolution of our consciousness, and it springs when we are reconnected with the truth—not the "truth" companies want us to believe or the "truth" advertisers spend millions to convince us of but the actual truth. We, as consumers, are pushing forward the very things we believe are wrong—all because we remain in the dark. We have unknowingly supported modern-day slavery, social injustice, racism, discrimination, and even environmental destruction with every poor buying decision that supports corporations, products, and practices that exploit people and the environment. *We essentially help these companies grow and, in the process, they exploit more people and the earth in the name of money.*

This is not a wake-up call. This is not a warning. *This is an international scream for action.* Our collective trust that all companies "will do the right thing" is a facade. And people are exploited in the most horrific way. Is it our fault? Absolutely not, yet once we know the truth, once we understand what is happening, then doing nothing makes us complicit in a crime that happens every second.

How many more items in your house need to be tainted by forced labor, child labor, or slave labor before you take a stance? One? Two? Ten? One hundred and forty-eight? *Not every company or item has slavery in its supply chain*, but it's enough of a problem that the U.S. Department of Labor releases a new report every year about the dangers of forced labor and slave labor in common products.[51] Specifically, the report refers to 148 commonly used goods from seventy-six countries.[52] These items are in every home and in every cupboard, refrigerator, and pantry across America. The most common items on the list are the following:

| | | | |
|---|---|---|---|
| cotton | sugarcane | carpets | gold |
| tea | fish | footwear | diamonds |
| rice | bananas | electronics | gems |
| shrimp | coffee | garments | fireworks |
| strawberries | bricks | rubber | toys |

Ironically, the items listed above don't even make up a *fraction* of the 148 commonly used items in your home that show up on this infamous list.[53] *The list shows which countries these items come from that are believed to use child labor or forced labor.*[54] So what does this mean for the average consumer? What can you do? More than you ever thought possible.

The revolution starts with you.

# CHAPTER FOUR

# BLOOD DIAMONDS

I n 2006, when the movie *Blood Diamond* was released, it took the world by storm. Most people had never heard of the terms *blood diamond*. Was this movie actually based on reality or just a new spin on a Hollywood storyline meant to capitalize on Leonardo DiCaprio's ever-growing popularity? The answers to those questions are an astonishing yes to both.

The $81 billion diamond industry faced a public relations apocalypse when the term *blood diamond* went mainstream after the movie was released by Warner Brothers. Ripples were felt across the luxury world of diamonds. Until the release of the movie, most people never knew that some of the world's most valuable stones were funding murders in war torn areas by rebel groups using forced labor and even slave labor in Africa.

Up until that point, *blood diamonds* and *conflict diamonds* had not become synonymous in the mainstream media. After watching the movie, millions of people finally began to understand how some diamonds were connected to the worst of humanity, a frightening intersection of modern-day slavery, bloody conflict, forced labor, discrimination, racism, and child labor in the middle of the struggle for power in some of the most unstable areas of the world.

Yet the diamond giants had known about this problem *at least six years before* the mainstream media would ever catch wind of it. In 2000, the biggest leaders in the diamond industry descended onto Kimberley, South Africa, in their private jets and first-class tickets with change on their minds. A potential consumer boycott over the uncut diamonds funding civil wars in Angola and Sierra Leone had brought the leaders together to brainstorm ideas and solutions. From that meeting, the Kimberley Process Certification Scheme was born.[55]

The Kimberley Process would essentially create a diamond travel system where uncut stones would have their own "travel passport" showing their country of origin. On paper it was nothing short of a brilliant idea. Official documents would follow the uncut diamonds so precious stones from conflict areas would be banned from entering international trade. Within three years of the first meeting in Kimberley, South Africa, over fifty governments, nonprofits, and advocacy groups accepted the new idea behind the Kimberley Process.[56]

Diamonds mined from war zones would be essentially shut out of the international diamond market, thereby creating a system where consumers could rest assured that their diamonds were not funding atrocities and murders overseas.

Even though the Kimberly Process was a giant leap in the right direction, critics argue it didn't go far enough to ensure that diamonds were ethically mined or that human trafficking, child labor, and/or forced labor were not in their supply chain.

First, the definition of a "conflict" diamond was so narrowly adopted in the Kimberley Process that even diamonds in some questionable areas and situations could still easily enter international trade. The definition of *conflict diamonds* was essentially gemstones sold to fund rebel movements attempting to overthrow the government.[57] That definition did not even begin to cover all the scenarios in which human rights and diamond mining intersect in a deadly way.

When a massacre of over two hundred miners, along with thousands of others raped, killed, or injured, occurred in Africa in 2008, the Kimberley Process was not violated since no rebel group was involved.[58]

Some leaders and consumers began to realize that mining the world's most precious stones, even outside of conflict areas, can be brutal, backbreaking work, often performed by low-paid workers under long hours and excruciating heat. Some of the miners are even black children who are denied the basic right to an education. Has the industry really climbed out of the public relations nightmare it faced back in 2000? The answer is surprisingly yes and no.

There is no debate that Africa is home to over 60 percent of the world's diamonds. It's easy to imagine that it would add to the continent's wealth. Yet at times it's been more of a curse than a blessing. Some smaller areas need the diamond industry so that residents can literally eat and sustain a basic livelihood.

Yet the opportunity for money does not absolve the industry of its obligation to ethically mine its diamonds or be free of human trafficking, child labor, or forced labor. Certain countries and leaders within the diamond industry have lobbied to expand the Kimberley Process to include *prohibitions against human rights violations and environmental degradation for diamond mining.* Some have even lobbied that only fair-labor diamonds should be allowed into the international market. But those efforts have been silenced, and questionable practices in mining diamonds still exist today, even outside war zones, where no rebel groups exist.

So it raises the question, Is human trafficking an ongoing problem in the glittering world of diamonds? The answer is yes. Yet the dispute is how much of a problem and whether any diamond can be ethically pure of human rights abuses and environmental degradation. It can be argued that many consumers are more interested in the labor practices behind the precious stones that symbolize their love than the carat, color, and clarity. The question is whether the diamond industry is truly listening and how far consumers will go to boycott diamonds that have questionable origins.

To solve some of these lingering problems, companies like Brilliant Earth and Allurez have emerged to start a new movement in the diamond industry by selling diamonds free of human rights abuses while promoting fair labor practices. Brilliant Earth's mission goes one step further and guarantees their diamonds are mined in an environmentally conscious and ethical way. They agree that the Kimberley Process's narrow definition leaves out "large numbers of diamonds that are tainted by violence, human rights abuses, poverty, and environmental degradation."[59] And their mission is to do something about it.

Yet it's not just new companies that are beginning to listen to socially conscious consumers. Industry icons like Tiffany & Co. and De Beers's Forevermark have been spearheading change within the diamond industry for years. These giants of the diamond world have instituted ethical sourcing in their mining of precious stones. Yet is that enough?

A flat boycott by consumers around the world would not change the industry overnight. Conscious consumers may want ethical diamonds, yet the real solution exists in expanding the Kimberley Process and organizing miners into cooperatives so they are partners in a system that encourages fair trade in a way that benefits everyone, especially the workers who mine the stones in Africa. The people who do the most difficult work of digging those precious metals shouldn't be the ones who benefit the least from the billion dollar industry.

A Fair Trade diamond certification system could help do for the diamond industry what it has done for coffee farmers around the world: avoid a serious boycott while fostering a system where those who need the proceeds and do the most work don't end up with the least.

After all, when did doing the right thing ever go out of style?

## The Dark Side of Fairy Tales

It can be easily stated that diamonds are to women what toys are to children, items to be admired, shown, and even celebrated. Yet, their connection doesn't end there. It's actually much deeper.

Just like in movies, children are immersed into a world of fairy tales through their toys. A world where good overcomes evil, heroines find their happily ever after, and the villain is destroyed.

These fairy tales play out in millions of households across the world through shiny toys. Yet fairy tales and the realities behind making certain toys are as different as night and day. It's a difference many people remain unaware of.

An investigation into labor conditions at five different Chinese toy factories by China Labor Watch[60] revealed workers toiling away in conditions highly hazardous to their physical and mental health.[61] The investigation discovered workers living under brutal management, working eleven hours each day for six days a week in conditions where some workers were not even allowed a bathroom or water break during a four-hour shift.[62] They also found examples of toy workers only able to visit their *own children* or families once a year just to make ends meet with the little pay they earned.[63]

During China Labor Watch's investigation, "a supplier factory to Hasbro, Mattel, and Walmart, experienced a strike of about 100 workers who demanded severance compensation and insurance back pay from the factory before its impending relocation. The action was ultimately unsuccessful, and some workers were detained by the police."[64]

Yet that wasn't even the most shocking discovery. China Labor Watch's investigation implicated the following toy companies: "Hasbro, Mattel, and Mattel-owned Fisher Price, McDonald's, Jakks Pacific, Disney, NSI Toys, Battat, and MGA Entertainment. Some of the toy brands observed during the investigation include Frozen, Monster High, Nerf, Marvel, Star Wars, Wubble Ball, Fur Real Friends, Hot Wheels, and Lalaloopsy."[65]

The toy brands categorically deny knowledge of such bad working conditions and insist they take every measure to make sure each toy is created in an ethical manner according to existing codes of conduct and standards. However, how can this be sustained when toy brands "play toy manufacturers off one another to reduce production prices and maximize profit margins," according to China Labor Watch?[66]

Two years after this report, China Labor Watch sent investigators to four more toy factories in China and found workers exposed to toxic chemicals, excessive overtime, and living in dormitory conditions that were substandard at best.[67] This begs the question, "When will it end?"

# CHAPTER FIVE

# FAST FASHION, MODERN-DAY SLAVERY, AND THE ENVIRONMENTAL FALLOUT

W hile consumers are bombarded with images of beautiful runway models on the catwalks of Paris, Milan, and New York, the fashion industry has a much darker side that remains hidden. One that designers and models wearing the latest collections barely ever talk about in public. The secret? The fashion industry is one of the greatest supporters and users of modern-day slavery and injustice today.[68]

This secret remains hidden in plain sight. Countries that are a part of the G20 bring in *$127 billion* worth of garments that are at risk of being tainted by slavery every year.[69] Forced labor, child labor, and/or slave labor can be present on every level of the fashion industry from the factories and countless sweatshops that make the clothes to the basic raw materials, such as cotton, that are harvested by adults and children denied a basic livable wage and safe working conditions.

These modern-day slaves often provide the backbone for the billion-dollar fashion industry but remain hidden behind the glamour of fashion week, runway models, and beautiful clothes—until now.

The United States and the developed world out consume clothes made by modern-day slavery. Even though states like California have created transparency laws that force companies to reveal their actions in fighting slavery in their supply chain, the law is only recognized in that state and exempts corporations with a global income of under $100 million,[70] which severely undercuts the point of having such legislation in the first place.

Once we know the industry's involvement in modern-day slavery and injustice, the fashion industry fears we will no longer see the glamorous images as truth but mere illusions. They are absolutely right. How can we when it's often built on the backbone of slavery or forced labor? How can we when our clothes are often made by people who are denied basic human rights? How can we when a basic truth is denied? Slavery in any country is a problem for every country. A moral failure on every level.

Over 40 million people live in slave-like conditions today, and too many of them are working in the supply chain of the clothes we wear and disregard every day.[71] According to the lifestyle brand ABLE, the fashion world is "one of the largest industrial employers of women worldwide, yet only an estimated 2% of fashion workers are paid a livable wage."[72] That means that 98 percent of fashion workers, the backbone of the industry, can't meet their basic needs.[73]

Do magazine spreads show the countless sweatshops or buildings around the world that house men, women, and children working twelve to sixteen hours a day making meager wages just to survive? Do we see that side of the fashion industry? Not a chance.

This raises the question, Is ignorance bliss? Is it better to remain unaware? The answer is unequivocally no, because the more we remain in the dark, the faster this problem grows. Not every fashion or clothing company has slave labor, forced labor, or child labor in their supply change. Many have avoided these serious issues by being more vigilant, but enough do not that makes it a problem that must be faced straight on.

For millions of us, a fun shopping day with friends or family can easily include coffee, chocolate, clothes, and food. Yet many never realize the connection to modern-day injustices and slavery in each of these industries. Until now.

Yet how did we get here? How did fast fashion and human trafficking become intertwined? How did the fashion industry become one of the greatest supporters of modern-day slavery and injustice today? Ultimately, how can we reverse this problem?

## The Explosion of Fast Fashion

The explosion of "fast fashion," as it would become so infamously known, began speeding forward at an unprecedented rate at the end of the 1990s.

Big chain retailers and brands like H&M, Forever21, and The Gap realized the old way of producing a handful of collections for winter, spring, summer, and fall only limited profits, while people were becoming increasingly obsessed with the newest styles on and off the runway.

This discovery, along with the growth of globalization, created an inevitable path for companies to ship their designs to underdeveloped countries, where labor and overhead costs were pennies on the dollar.

Before the 1960s, almost 95 percent of our clothes were made in America. With the explosion of fast fashion, the pendulum completely shifted and created a new reality where only 3 percent of clothes were actually made here, while 97 percent were outsourced around the world. This new reality created the perfect storm for a problem that consumers would unknowingly support and expand. This crossroads resulted in the explosion of fast fashion and its intersection with human rights, yet most of the outside world remained completely unaware.

With low overhead costs, retailers and brands began multiplying the number of collections shipped to stores each year. Fast fashion gained speed and profits, but the quality and the process of creating clothes were coming into question. If items were being created so quickly and cheaply, how could high quality be guaranteed? And ultimately, who was really paying the ultimate price for the "lower" cost? Consumers? Workers? What was the truth behind the growth of the fast fashion movement, and would it come to a head with human rights?

More importantly, when would people begin to realize it, if ever?

Consumers remained blissfully unaware of what was happening behind the scenes. What they did realize was their favorite stores no longer received a handful of new styles every year. Some stores were gaining merchandise every month, and this lag time would increasingly become shortened to two weeks.

The increase in the fast fashion cycle generated more interest from style-conscious fashionistas who were looking for the latest trends at the lowest prices. A perfect storm was in place for a fashion revolution, where workers would be the victims and consumers would become the unwitting co-conspirators in a bid to increase profits. Yet at what cost? And what would it take to create a new model for fashion that wouldn't continue to exploit basic human rights?

## Fast Fashion's Environmental Footprint

This fashion revolution wasn't just impacting human rights globally. New methods for creating fast fashion began affecting the environment as well. While the environment and fashion are not commonly linked together, the reality is far from the truth.

*Fashion is the second-most polluting industry in the world, not nationally but globally.* The only other industry that pollutes the world more is the oil industry. Fashion with its quick turnaround and harmful effects on rivers, lakes, landfills, and air quality is slowly catching up to the oil industry.

The truth is hard to deny: fast fashion has left a damaging impact on the environment. And many fashion-obsessed retailers and buyers remain unaware of how their love of clothes is destroying the earth, polluting the world, and leaving a negative footprint for generations to come.

Our planet cannot replenish itself at the pace of our consumption, and the exploitation of natural resources needed to make fast fashion is creating a disastrous crossroads. From the questionable supply chains to the exploitation of raw materials used to make the clothes and toxic waste produced from dyeing practices, toxic chemicals from textile factories are too often released into the surrounding waters, emitting toxins like arsenic, mercury, and lead into rivers and surrounding areas. These environmental toxins not only damage underdeveloped countries that make these clothes but also pollute the surrounding waters, which remain untreated and surge into the ocean.

The result is disastrous. The majority of China's bodies of water are unfit for drinking and even bathing because of all the industrial toxins that have been dumped into them. Each time we buy and throw away fast fashion, we contribute to the destruction of marine life, oceans, rivers, and air, as well as filling landfills that continue to contaminate the earth for decades.

Sadly, it doesn't stop there. In the process of creating two of the most common materials in fast fashion, polyester and nylon, greenhouse gases are emitted into the air, contributing to the problem of global warming. This release of these gases into the atmosphere is over three times more harmful than carbon dioxide. The fashion industry is responsible for 10 percent of all carbon emissions around the world contributing to the problem of climate change.

Our high rate of consumption doesn't help. It's no secret that most people wear less than a quarter of the clothes in their wardrobe, leaving 75 percent of their clothes sitting in closets, often set aside for the ten to twenty pounds they may, or may not, lose in the future.

The more clothes people buy, the more clothes they throw away, which has led to the real problem of *fashion landfills*. Landfills filled with millions of tons of clothing that have dire environmental consequences. Wool garments decompose in landfills and produce methane as a by-product, a leading contributor to global warming, while man-made fibers do not decompose, creating their own unique set of problems for the environment—not to mention the excess fuel and resources wasted every year to ship fast fashion from one side of the world to the other to be bought and sold and ultimately thrown away.

Fast fashion has become an environmental disaster as well as a serious human rights problem. Our fashion choices have profound social impact and meaning, and until consumers begin to realize this hidden connection, our waste will continue to pollute the air, rivers, lakes, oceans, and marine life at a devastating rate while adding to global warming.

Change is happening, albeit slowly. Some retailers are beginning to act more responsibly. H&M has started a Conscious Collection, while shoe giant Nike has created a shoe-recycling program; but for the environmental footprint of fast fashion to have a positive impact change is needed across the board in ways that will decrease the negative footprint of fashion while providing workers a livable wage with safe working conditions. Is this possible? Absolutely, and that change can't happen fast enough.

Ultimately, it's consumers that can foster change by demanding more from their favorite brands and calling for reform and transparency across the industry that is meaningful and benefits the backbone of the fashion world: the workers who harvest and make the beautiful clothes we wear every day.

After all, fashion is a form of self-expression. It's how we present ourselves to the world. It's used to convey who we are, our style, and even our personalities. Then why can't it convey our values as well?

# CHAPTER SIX

# ELECTRONICS

I t's no secret the Magnificent Mile in Chicago attracts shoppers from all over the world. It's every shopping enthusiast's dream come true, with flagship stores from Apple, Burberry, Nike, Macy's, H&M, and Barnes & Noble (just to name a few) all lined up along one long, beautiful road in the most exclusive part of Michigan Avenue.

On a hot, humid day in the summer of 2012, I was one of those shopping enthusiasts strategically maneuvering around the scores of tourists coming right at me. Before getting lost in the crowd, I slipped into the Apple flagship store. Its translucent doors immediately caught my attention.

From the outside, there is no building more transparent than the Apple store, with its walls of glass as the storefront. As I opened the glass doors, the song "Shine Bright Like a Diamond," by Rihanna, blared through the speakers. The lyrics seem fitting for a store and a brand that attracted buyers from around the world with undying loyalty.

Within moments, a friendly Apple employee approached me in his pressed corporate-blue shirt and wide smile. He politely asked if this was my first time to the store. I nodded and told him that I was only there to browse. As if on cue, he began listing their new products from memory as I gazed absentmindedly around the store to see dozens of people crowded around beautiful white oak tables, peering at the new iPads that line the edges of the desks.

The irony hit me immediately. The matching white oak floors and tables next to glass walls in the middle of the store conveyed a sense of transparency. For a moment, I stopped and wondered, how much of this is actually true? How transparent is Apple? Have they always been transparent? Do these consumers ever wonder who actually makes these products? And if they did, would it matter to them at all?

As I looked around, I noticed more than one hundred people peering contentedly into Apple products. I'm reminded of the 137 factory workers in China injured in 2009 after being forced to use poisonous chemicals to clean new iPhone screens. After that incident, two explosions at iPad factories killed 4 workers and injured 77 more. Both have been widely reported by media outlets and advocacy groups outside China.

These statistics ran through my mind as I peered up slowly to examine the transparent glass stairway in the middle of the store. I began to wonder, "How different are those workers from the people in this store today, leisurely spending their Saturday afternoon looking at new Apple products?"

Unbeknownst to millions, these coveted products connect us to lives across the world that have been shortened or lost in the process of making them. Even one life lost is too many. Yet accusations of human rights violations include more than injuries or deaths. In May 2012, Students and Scholars Against Corporate Misbehavior reported that on average eight workers who made Apple products lived in a three-bedroom apartment.[74] They are considered the lucky ones. In the "processing-zone campus" in Zhengzhou, China, the same group reported that workers live in dormitory apartments that house up to thirty people.[75]

Were the people in the flagship store aware of these reports? Would they even care? As I contemplate these questions, I absentmindedly leaned on a white oak table and glance over to see a man in his fifties frantically typing away at a new Apple computer with a forty-inch screen. I decided to approach him to test my theory, whether human lives matter more than our ability to access the best and newest technology.

After I introduced myself, I began to ask him an array of questions, from his occupation to his loyalty toward the Apple brand. Within a matter of minutes, I discovered that he was a doctor, a specialist from Minneapolis who had come to Chicago for a weekend getaway with his family.

"I have owned every Apple product since the eighties," Dr. J. Mayford[76] proudly told me. He then began to list off the superiority of the brand and how these products "can't be found anywhere else." To end his ten-minute Apple admiration monologue, he concluded that he used Apple products to save lives in his medical practice as a tool in patient education.

After listening to his impressive monologue, I finally asked the question I've been dying to ask since I stepped into the glass store. "Are you aware of the human rights allegations made against Apple?" His eyes squint as he adjusted his coat and looked around uncomfortably. He takes a deep breath and tells me that he had read the media articles and found it impossible to believe.

"It's not like they are involved in slave labor," Dr. Mayford said with a smirk. Before I had a chance to question that statement, his son approached. "Well, I really must get going," he said. Before he left, I asked one more question. "If it was hypothetically close to slave labor, would it impact your purchasing decision in any way?"

The man who took the oath to do no harm stopped for a moment and unconvincingly said, "No." He explained that because the products were so superior and helpful, he would still buy Apple technology regardless of how it was made. He left by saying, "I am a die-hard, loyal Apple fanatic. You should know that."

As he walked away, I turned around to watch him leave. For a moment, I was stunned by his response, but then I remembered something I had been told years ago. One voice can either turn a blind eye to oppression and injustice or shine a light on a problem that is greatly misunderstood. The white, privileged doctor did not want to hear my words, but in my heart, I knew millions of others would.


## OUR SEEMINGLY INNOCENT DAILY CHOICES

From the electronics we use to the clothes we wear; consumer choices have wide-reaching social consequences whether we want to admit it or not. Those were the words I wanted to tell the good doctor but never had a chance to. Far beyond the world we live in, our choices can either help continue a problem or help to stop it.

The human rights allegations against Apple have been well documented online and in the media. In response, Apple has stepped up its efforts to combat the problem. They admit that their supply chain is global and so is their responsibility.[77]

According to their website, "Apple products are made all over the world. We work with suppliers, from mining to recycling, to verify that our requirements are being met for the people and communities in our supply chain. In 2018, a total of 1049 supplier assessments were conducted in 45 countries."[78]

They go on to say that Apple "care[s] deeply about the people who build our products, and the planet we all share. So we hold ourselves and our suppliers to the highest standards to ensure everyone is treated with dignity and respect. And we share our work openly so others can follow our lead."[79]

Apple has made significant progress forward, and they showcase it in their 2019 Progress Report;[80] yet, as they eloquently state, "We believe that if we're not finding areas to improve, we're not looking hard enough."[81]

The great news about Apple is they recognize the problems associated with human rights and the environment and are dealing with it head-on by auditing the companies they work with to make iPhones and iPads around the world. (For more information, see Apple's 2019 Progress Report.)

In Apple's internal audit of 2018, twenty-seven core violations were discovered out in the open regarding human rights. These included twenty-four cases of falsification of employees' working hours, one child labor case, and two debt-bonded violations.[82] The company worked to investigate and fix these violations, as all companies should. Apple's efforts are highly commendable and necessary, yet the problem of human rights violations often occur hidden away, and the U.S. government has started its own audits to uncover it.

## A NEW WORLD

It's no surprise that the world closely watches what companies like Apple, Samsung, and Sony create and ship out to every corner of the globe, but the U.S. Department of Labor also watches from afar, knowing that modern-day slavery and factories making the latest electronics can be more connected than people may realize.

The supply chain of electronics is vast and circles the globe. To help uncover the truth, the U.S. Department of Labor commissioned Verité, an independent and nonprofit organization, to study and investigate the claims of forced labor in the up-and-coming manufacturing mecca of electronics known as Malaysia.[83]

Malaysia has become a global hub for the manufacturing of electronics. Called the "Silicon Island of the East," Penang was the new center for electronics manufacturing.[84] In 2013, almost a third of all jobs created in the country of Malaysia were from manufacturing electronics alone, while some of the most recognizable brands around the world can be connected back to Malaysia.[85]

To promote this growth and development, the Malaysian government created eighteen free industrial zones, which provide many benefits to companies via tax breaks and duty-free import of raw materials for manufacturing.[86]

The Malaysian government views electronics manufacturing as a key driving force in the nation's developing economy and for good reason. While investors see a robust opportunity for money and profits, human rights activists see a world where human rights can be exploited for greater profit, a dangerous intersection of greed and human exploitation that can spread quickly in an environment of secrecy. That is why the U.S. Department of Labor's interest in the electronics sector in Malaysia was so necessary and timely. Lives were literally depending on it.

It can be argued that Verité's report was nothing less than a bomb imploding within the electronics industry. No one knew exactly what the research would uncover, and some were ready to deny it before the conclusions were ever released. However, to deny the results, one would first have to understand them and how the secret world of electronics manufacturing and human trafficking were somehow connected. Not all electronics made in Malaysia could be traced back to modern-day slavery. But it was enough of a problem that activists around the world began to take notice.

Hundreds of thousands of foreign workers flocked to Malaysia on the promise of good jobs and steady income in the coveted electronics industry. Like all people, they hoped for a better life for themselves and their family back home. Given that Malaysia is such a small country, the electronics industry needed outside labor to flourish. It seemed like such a great fit on paper. Yet the shocking part was the number of migrant workers who were found to live in forced labor conditions while paying back the "fees" that helped land them in Malaysia in the first place:

> The fees workers' pay to different agents [who help them get the jobs in Malaysia]…are often high, and in many cases family land must be leveraged or a loan taken in order to pay the fee. These fees can vary widely by country of

origin and are commonly above legal limits set
by sending countries and receiving countries.
Fees charged by local sub-agents and recruitment agents in sending countries are unregulated and often leave a worker in debt before
they have arrived in Malaysia.[87]

For some, their indebtedness and unforeseen introduction
to the world of forced labor began even before setting foot in
Malaysia. By creating a non-uniform system where people pay
varying amounts for recruitment fees to get jobs, it created vul-
nerability for migrant workers already far from home. Instead
of coming in and making money, some start work already in
debt and remain in debt for months and even years to come.

While some of the third-party employment agents do provide a valuable resource to the companies by offering a pool
of potential workers, others take advantage of their role by
charging too much or creating a system where paying back
the agency can take longer than was originally anticipated.[88]
Until a uniform system of fees and recruiting practices is created systematically across the board, there will always be the
potential for unscrupulous agents to take advantage of foreign
workers trying to better their lives.

Yet that was just the beginning. Over a quarter of the foreign workers interviewed in the study reported they could not
move around freely outside their preselected housing. They
were watched via surveillance as they went to work and returned home while also being segregated by the rest of the
public.[89] Not all workers lived in this manner, but it was enough

of a problem that those in these circumstances reported feeling isolated on top of being followed.

Many of those interviewed for the report rarely left their hostels because they feared being stopped by police, an issue further exacerbated by the fact that many were forced to give up their passports to their employers or agents at the beginning of their employment.[90] For too many workers, a bleak picture was revealed to the world, and the rest of the findings would do little to put human rights activists' minds at ease.

The issue wasn't whether forced labor existed in the electronics industry in Malaysia. This study and its predecessors (Amnesty International, Center for Research on Multinational Corporations, National Human Rights Commission) had all uncovered that forced labor did exist.[91] The bigger question was to what extent did forced labor touch the lives of the electronics we use, and would the truth be stranger than fiction?

Yet the statistics were not what shocked human rights activists. The stories coming out of the U.S. commissioned study started to reveal the picture of what was happening and why this issue was just beginning to grow. Quotes from the report by actual participants began to paint a picture for some living in the electronics sector of Malaysia:

> This is a terrible life. I would have never come here if I had known that this is what I would go through. Luck has not favored me. I can't even return to my home country because I don't have my passport.—*Male Burmese worker in Klang Valley.*[92]

She [the respondent] says that workers have had to help each other when one of them falls ill. She says that a common problem experienced by workers is very low blood pressure and fainting during work hours. She says that this is probably because workers do not get much sleep. With 12 hours of work every day, and having to prepare meals, line up for the toilet and bathroom use, and being in the factory grounds 45 minutes before start of work, there is actually very little time for sleep and rest.—*Verité researcher, describing interview with female Vietnamese worker in Penang.*[93]

Our employer forces us to work seven days a week. I am exhausted. I stand for 12 hours every day. If we don't work, our employer beats us. I have seen a Nepalese worker beaten. The employer also beat a Vietnamese worker and cut her hair.—*Female Vietnamese worker in Penang.*[94]

Normally I work from Monday to Saturday. Sunday depends on my health. When the factory is busy, we have to work 16 hours.—*Female Vietnamese worker in Penang.*[95]

These quotes represent some of the worst stories coming out of Malaysia. Not all participants expressed having a difficult life. Some had found a way to work, live, and send money back to their families. Some had found a chance at a better future.

But the success stories were not the ones bothering human rights activists. The ones who described a life of forced labor, bad working and living conditions are the ones whose stories got the attention of activists around the world. The conditions of some foreign workers in the Malaysian electronics industry had received attention from international organizations way before the report from Verité.

Research from Amnesty International,[96] a German organization,[97] and a Netherlands[98] based company had already documented the lives of foreign workers in the electronics sector. For some, the news of the conditions coming out of Malaysia were no surprise. For others, it detailed a dark secret behind the electronics industry that needed to be fixed. Not every electronics company in Malaysia (or around the world) deal with these issues, but it was enough of a concern for some companies that people began to take notice.

The Verité study made it clear that researchers and authors of the report had used very rigid standards to find the prevalence of forced labor, and as a result their numbers "are very likely lower than the actual rate of forced labor in the Malaysian electronics industry and should be viewed as a minimum estimate."[99] They found the rate of forced labor was as high as 48 percent among workers who were indebted for their recruitment fees. The overall percentage in the sample study showed that over a quarter of the participants were in forced labor (at a very minimum). When Malaysian citizens were taken out of the sample group, then the rate increased to 32 percent.[100]

The report had one goal, to give a voice to the workers who had "bravely and altruistically shared their personal experiences, knowing that they would not experience any direct or immediate improvement in their lives from the study, but in the hopes that the shared understandings emerging from the research would serve as a catalyst for change."[101]

This is why the Red Movement is so vital. It helps people understand how our seemingly innocent unchecked consumerism adds to the problem of slavery, social injustice, child labor, forced labor, and environmental degradation far beyond the small corner of the world we each live in. Collectively we have been kept in the dark about how technological devices and fashion (two of the most common everyday purchases on the planet) have cost people and the environment.

The time for change is now. The "need" to buy the best and most current version isn't making us happier. It's making us more dissatisfied with what we already have by feeding into the false idea that the next big product or item will bring us closer to joy, when that joy is based on something very temporary. Just like an addict, we are chasing a high that will always come to an abrupt end. Our obsession with "Keeping Up with the Joneses" is feeding our unhappiness and sense of emptiness.

At what point is our obsession with having the best or the latest gadget enough? And how does that obsession intersect with human rights and the kind of environmental degradation the world has never seen before? It's all connected in ways few may realize. Until now.

# CHAPTER SEVEN

# HOW DID WE GET HERE?

*If companies are unwilling or unable to pay a fair living wage,*
*then they shouldn't be doing business.*
*Expecting humans to work at or below poverty levels*
*so that businesses can make huge profits is privilege at its absolute*
*worse*
*regardless of where the workers live.*

## REALITY VERSUS PERCEPTION: THE ILLUSION UNRAVELS

Marketers love consumers who remain in the dark because they are the biggest supporters of modern-day slavery, social injustice, and environmental destruction today. Unchecked consumerism helps some brands make billions of dollars every year while consumers remain unaware of how their purchasing power impacts the earth.

Some corporations want this to continue. Why? Because consumers often believe the perception of a product over the harsh reality, and that in turn leads to rising revenues. It has for decades, and it continues today.

The products that use slave labor, child labor, or forced labor in the U.S. Department of Labor's, *List of Goods Produced by Child Labor or Forced Labor,* is as daunting as the list of countries they are produced in, from garments to grapes, olives, strawberries, bricks, carpets, sugarcane, tomatoes, cotton—the list goes on for pages.[102] It's a laundry list of supplies found in every home today.[103]

How did this vicious cycle begin? And why hasn't it stopped? To understand the explosion of these problems and how we, as consumers, are contributing to these dangerous trends, we have to understand the rise of unchecked consumerism. We have to go back to the beginning, before *need* and *want* became synonymous in our "Keeping Up with the Joneses"–obsessed world.

## THE BIRTH OF UNCHECKED CONSUMERISM

In the first half of the 1900s, consumerism was driven by survival. Once consumption levels started to outpace actual human needs, we began to see the very real and serious problems that exist today.

Long before Apple learned how to create an international frenzy with the launch of their latest iPhone, consumption had real-life survival consequences. Before and shortly after the turn of the twentieth century, most families bought only what they needed. They saved up for the essentials for months and even years. They didn't take out loans, max-out credit cards, or buy on impulse. Consumerism was not linked to status, identity, or happiness. It was linked to survival.

People adopted ideas fundamentally different from what we see today. What they owned, possessed, or bought did not necessarily define who or where they were in life. And it definitely didn't add meaning to it. A bigger wardrobe did not mean a happier life. A thousand shoes did not demonstrate higher status or wealth. A larger house did not automatically translate into success. In fact, these things were thought of as wasteful and extravagant—two words we rarely hear in the "shop till you drop" culture we live in now.

Americans weren't always unchecked consumers. This desire did not come innately or intuitively. Like most habits, it's learned behavior. The history of unchecked (also known as unconscious) consumerism really began at the end of World War I. Why does this matter? Because it has contributed to the growth of modern-day slavery, injustice, racism, discrimination and the environmental fallout in ways people have never realized. Back then, corporations were coming out of an era of overproduction and increased profit. The problem of supply exceeding demand was a real threat to corporate prosperity, and that threat was a problem for rich businessmen around the nation. This is when unconscious consumerism was born. Unbeknownst to millions, banker Paul Mazur, of Lehman Brothers, would have an iconic role in its creation, without realizing the long-term consequences.

"We must shift America from a need, to a desires culture," wrote Mazur.[104] "People must be trained to desire, to want new things even before the old had been entirely consumed. We must shape a new mentality in America. Man's desires must overshadow his needs."[105]

Along with this major shift in thinking, a new form of advertising began to emerge to keep corporations from going bankrupt since supply was exceeding demand. Prior to this shift, everything from cars to appliances were marketed towards rational buyers who consumed purely what they needed.

Now corporations were going to make buyers want things they didn't actually need by connecting "things" to unconscious desires to increase sales. Now cars were not only marketed for their efficiency but also for their symbol of status, sexuality, and dominance.

The concept of the unconscious was central to Sigmund Freud's account of the mind. While Sigmund Freud was making contributions to psychology by writing and studying about the unconscious mind, his nephew, Edward Bernays, would use the same knowledge to show corporations how to make money. He would show the magic of selling unneeded products to feed people's unconscious desires.

Edward Bernays became the father of product placement and claims he was the first to teach big corporations how to sell items as symbols instead of necessities for survival.[106] That became one of the biggest shifts in marketing history.

Around this time, an American journalist noted that "a change has come over our democracy, it is called consumptions. The American citizen first importance to his country is no longer that of citizen, but that of consumer."[107]

The first U.S. President to include the role of consumerism in American culture and encourage its growth was elected in 1928. It's been famously noted that President Herbert Hoover told a group of key public relations officials and elite advertisers, "You have taken over the job of creating desire and have transformed people into constantly moving happiness machines. Machines which have become the key to economic progress."[108]

Years later, the haunting questions would arise: At whose expense? And at what price? And so the idea of unconscious consumerism began as a strategy to help big corporations avoid failure. Yet what the fathers of this new trend did not anticipate was the push-back that would rattle the country. While President Hoover and the titans of business were celebrating the boom in business, stocks began to plummet. Within a few days, the U.S. stock market would crash on October 29th 1929, creating a rippling effect felt by Americans and the entire world.

Suddenly people realized why the needs-based culture had been so beneficial. Families all over the nation had no choice but to go back to the basics and view consumerism as a tool for basic survival, not status or happiness.

While this was unfolding, the corporate leaders of the nation were not going to sit back quietly while their profits dwindled and their companies began to disappear into the abyss of bankruptcy. Public relations campaigns were aggressively launched. Once again, the engine that drove unconscious consumerism started to rattle, and it wasn't going to stop.

However, it would take until World War II for business leaders to receive the international push they so desperately needed to increase their revenue again. And when World War II was over, the movement for unconscious consumerism began raging ahead at a frightening speed. And that speed has continued to increase every decade since then.

Once unchecked (or unconscious) consumerism took hold of the American people, it began to embed itself in ways that have become a part of the culture. "Keeping up with the Joneses" was a mentality started in 1925 and by all accounts contributed to America's drive for unconscious consumption. Now it wasn't a matter of buying only necessities; it was a matter of keeping up appearances for the sake of superficial markers to show status, success, and happiness.

During World War II, advertisers carefully promoted products that would be available once the war ended. This created a sense of anticipation for consumers that peace and new products were intertwined with the opportunity for a better life. In the 1950s, credit cards were advertised as a time-saver, as opposed to a mechanism that created mounting debt for families who couldn't afford the items.

Fast-forward twenty years, and companies began to realize that if they outsourced their production to underdeveloped countries, then profits would explode. Now they had consumers buying things they didn't need from outsourced third world workers who were being paid, in some instances, pennies on the dollar.

Paying drastically lower wages to third-world workers became the next turn in making some corporations even richer than ever before, and it began a new wave of prosperity for them, while millions of people would be potentially exploited in the process on both sides of the world.

## BLACK LIVES MATTER, CONSUMERISM, AND MODERN-DAY SLAVERY

At the time that globalization was beginning to take effect it was having a serious impact on various communities both expectedly and unexpectedly. Jobs began to disappear from urban areas since corporations were now moving production to third world counties.

At the time, many didn't realize that this would devastate black communities who relied on those jobs to feed their families. In 1954, the unemployment rate for young black and white communities were relatively equal with the black communities having slightly better employment numbers than their white counterpart.

Once globalization started to gain traction the unemployment rate for young black men began rising. In the 1980's the unemployment rate for black men rose almost four times more than their white counterpart. Urban factories began to close their doors as companies decided third world workers would provide more work for less pay.

Globalization and deindustrialization would result in a higher percentage of black men losing their jobs while the nation began to shift to a service-oriented economy. This was devastating for minority communities who saw their jobs slip away without any meaningful new work or educational opportunities, further leading to the economic breakdown of inner cities.

Instead of launching a war on poverty to help inner city families transition to this different global economy that was forming, the government launched a war on drugs that would further devastate these communities. Instead of pumping money into these communities for job training, educational assistance, or assistance for relocation avenues to help young black men find new employment, the government pumped money into law enforcement with a crackdown on the "war on drugs" with emphasize in the inner cities.

Between losing their jobs and facing an unknown future with little job prospects, these confluence of events would result in the mass incarceration of black men and a movement created decades later called Black Lives Matter to undue that injustice. Michelle Alexander, a legal scholar and civil rights attorney would point out that the war on drugs created by the government resulted in disproportional mass incarceration of young black men even though studies showed that their white counterparts were using and selling drugs at a similar rate.[109] Leading some civil rights advocates to say, "Where was the mass incarceration of white men for the same drug offenses?"

The criminal justice system would further devastate these minority communities by moving towards a more punitive approach with mandatory sentencing for drug offenses instead of taking a rehabilitative approach that we see today (in the opiate crisis). This unfairness fed into this cycle of injustice where white men were being prosecuted at much lower rates for similar crimes as their black counterparts. Instead of helping them out of poverty, the war on drugs led police departments to become more militarized and a boom in prison populations erupted that continues today.

If a war on poverty had been launched instead of a war on drugs, it's easy to correlate that the mass incarceration of black men wouldn't have become one of the most pressing social injustices of the 21st century. The racial aspect of mass incarceration is the most troubling and at the heart of the Black Lives Matter Movement. The United States imprisons more people including racial or ethnic minorities than any other country in the globe.[110] Even the most oppressive governments incarcerate less people than America.[111]

Opponents argue that any incarcerations were to make the public safer. Yet, the mass incarceration of black men didn't make society safer,[112] it just grouped a generation of men into a system that would legally discrimination against them even after they fulfilled their obligation to society by satisfying their sentences.

Instead of helping these groups reintegrate into society, laws were introduced in the 1990's that made it legal to deny felons the right to vote, the right to housing, the right to get an education through financial assistance, and other basic human rights. Discriminating against a group that had already lost their jobs, their families, and their communities was now the recourse of the criminal justice system through the enactment of new laws that essentially made a generation of black men second class citizens in their own country. And some wondered why the backlash would be so strong? It could be reasonably argued, it was long overdue.

## When Will It Finally End?

Slowly but surely, unchecked consumerism would become like a drug for the masses and began to change our society in subtle and not so subtle ways.

Robert Lane took this idea further and noted that if people became dependent on the products the factories created, then they would be less critical of the unfair working conditions the workers lived under.[113] *And sadly, he was completely right.* Strategically this was a brilliant move, according to Stewart Ewen, since people's unhappiness could be channeled toward buying rather than social justice or political protest[114] or other injustices (such as mass incarcerations) born out of this new global economy.

Modern advertisers were distracting consumers away from their problems and toward acquisition. The message was clear: Want a good life? Buy something new. Consumerism was being marketed as a way to solve unhappiness or frustration, even if only for a day. Yet the fact remained that the unhappiness or frustration consumers were escaping was often born out of the financial debt they accumulated while participating in this new global economy, a vicious cycle millions of people experience to this day.

Yet this "good life" was too often built on the backs of factory workers and children, who toiled for over twelve hours a day in often unsafe and unsanitary factories, making products that consumers didn't need and couldn't really afford. By paying workers pennies on the dollar and exploiting their need to make a living, some big corporations found their new gold rush with the help of unconscious consumerism. And the connection between mass incarceration, globalization, and unchecked consumerism would only be discovered decades later if ever.

In the meantime, a new environmental crisis was looming in the background since over 90 percent of the items used by Americans were created somewhere else. Aside from agriculture, these vast productions made in factories release harmful chemicals into the air, water, and soil.

Problems such as ozone depletion, water pollution, soil erosion, forest destruction, and air pollution could all be directly linked back to the massive job of supporting unconscious consumption. The level of greenhouse gases coming from the emissions of factories making the endless garments that people wear and dispose of has increased. Essentially, we became a "throwaway" culture, where every item is disposable without realizing the environmental consequences.

For example, the sheer amount of plastics produced and disposed between 2000 to 2010 alone was more than the total amount of plastic created in the *entire last century*. The amount of plastics the public throws away is mind-numbing. Oceans and waterways are becoming polluted with these plastics, and studies show that the number of marine life forms dying with plastics inside of them is rising dramatically. This devastation doesn't even include the greenhouse gases that are released by plastics, which contribute to climate change.[115]

The intersection of consumption, human rights, and the environment is unprecedented and has led some to search for other ways to find contentment that abandons our "throwaway" culture. One such idea, known as the KonMari method, has taken the world by storm. It's a system of simplifying and decluttering homes by keeping only items that bring people joy. As a result, people find that they don't need so much "stuff."

A simpler lifestyle that rejects the clutter our "throwaway" culture has created is booming in popularity. People across the globe are realizing that unchecked consumerism not only hurts the planet and workers but often leads to lives that are unfulfilling, overwhelming, and ridden with debt.

In other words, "Keeping Up with the Joneses" is making us miserable. That is why the Red Movement is so vital. Our consumption impacts not only our lives but the lives of others and the environment in ways few realize until now. This leads to the inevitable question, "What can be done, and who will lead the way?"

# PART II:

# HUMAN RIGHTS AND SPORTING EVENTS

# CHAPTER EIGHT

# THE SECRET BEHIND
# THE SUPER BOWL

*We've just hit the beginning*
*to understanding social injustices*
*that have been ignored far too long.*

Yet, labor problems and their environmental connections are just a part of the greater social injustices facing us today. Sex trafficking has become just as prevalent and damaging. In 2014, as the nation eagerly awaited the Super Bowl championship game between the Seattle Seahawks and Denver Broncos, the FBI prepared for one of their largest sting operations to date.[116] Millions of die-hard sports fans had no idea the two events were closely related.

Some spectators initially called the Super Bowl's hidden connection to modern-day slavery and human trafficking an urban legend while the FBI worked with over fifty law enforcement agencies for six months to rescue women and children from a cycle of abuse during, before, and after the big game.[117]

While people bought tickets for the biggest day in American sports, FBI Agents strategically mapped out areas to raid and intercept before, during, and after the big game to rescue children and teenagers (thirteen- to seventeen-year-old girls) ushered into empty hotel rooms around the MetLife Stadium in New Jersey. To unsuspecting eyes, the girls had arrived to celebrate the time-honored tradition of football, but behind the celebration was a much darker and sinister side.

"High-profile special events, which draw large crowds, have become lucrative opportunities for child prostitution criminal enterprises," said Ron Hosko, Assistant Director of the FBI's Criminal Investigative Division.[118] And young black girls have been disproportionately impacted by this problem.

What millions of unsuspecting fans never realized was that a shadow underground world has unknowingly emerged alongside America's favorite pastime. This hidden world has continued to grow and become all too familiar for thousands of girls who go missing or run away every day. And this has disproportionately impacted the African American communities. The statistics on human trafficking and African American women are shocking:

- *African American human trafficking numbers are among the highest in the country*

- *52% of all juvenile prostitution arrests are African Americans*

- *40% of victims of human trafficking are African Americans*[119]

Thousands of these women and children are trafficked to and from high-profile events like the Super Bowl, the Olympics, and the World Cup. To understand the problem of human trafficking, the United Nations defined it as the recruitment, transportation, or transfer of a person by improper and illegal methods (such as deception, threats, coercion, fraud, force, or abduction) for sexual exploitation, prostitution, or forced labor.[120] This is a modern-day form of slavery, where children as young as nine are recruited and lured into prostitution.

In the United States, any minor who is pulled into prostitution is considered a victim of human trafficking according to state and federal laws. The explosion of social media has made it easier for traffickers to find and recruit young girls into this dangerous world. Behind a computer screen, victims have no idea who they are really talking to.[121]

While Instagram and other social media apps have been used to deceive unsuspecting girls into an "easy business deal," other websites like Facebook have also been targeted to find teenagers.[122] It often starts as a simple Friend Request. A friendship slowly evolves and turns into something entirely different right at home, underneath the parents' watchful eyes.

Traffickers have also exploited the popularity of the gaming world. Xbox and PlayStation have been used to lure new "recruits" or "members" by giving predators instant access to children. Traffickers don't need to stroll through malls to lure children. All they need is a game console and the ability to play games.

Popular games such as *Fortnite* and *Minecraft* have been used to foster friendships, which can take days or months. Predators attract children by allowing them to win and gaining their trust over time. They slowly talk to children and offer a sympathetic ear after disagreements or conflicts with family members.

Stories have emerged where traffickers have persuaded children to run away or meet them outside the home.[123]

The majority of people in the gaming world have good intentions and are there merely to play. Yet many parents are unaware of the strangers who are invited into their homes on a daily basis via computers and game consoles. Unfortunately, technology is only one avenue for predators to find their prey.

## SASHA'S STORY—ONE OF A MILLION STOLEN LIVES

Like thousands of girls before her, Sasha[124] knew nothing about human trafficking or modern-day slavery. She had never even heard of those words before it took over her life.

Sasha's life would have unexpected twists and turns, but it all began outside of Chicago. Her Mother fondly remembered a fun-loving three year old little girl who randomly fell into fits of laughter. From a young age, Sasha loved to stand in front of her mother's full-length mirror with lipstick smeared across her face while imagining her wedding day. She fantasized about a day filled with laughter, celebration, and tears of joy. As she walked down the aisle, in her childlike imagination, she pictured a white, transparent veil flowing next to her dark hair. She could see the joy in her family's eyes. Just like the movies, she too would get her happy ending.

## THE BEGINNING

As Sasha entered junior high, she became an energetic teenager who loved sports and singing in the church choir. She experienced the same anxiety most teenagers go through. She desperately wanted to fit in and make new friends while maintaining a sense of independence. Her parents had moved to a new town, and she didn't know who she could trust. In many ways, her story remained common until she began high school. That's when her path took an unexpected detour.

At fifteen, she was beginning to navigate her new life in a different school. It was an uncertain time for any young girl who felt awkward and invisible. A crush on a senior would lead to an unexpected friendship after he invited her to a party.

"I remember being excited and not knowing what to wear. Looking back, that was the least of my worries." When she arrived at the party, he welcomed her with a smile. "I started to really feel like I was fitting in for the first time in my life."

She observed the upperclassmen while a boy offered her a drink in a red plastic cup. "It was really innocent in the beginning. There wasn't anything to worry about." She took the drink and began to relax.

Throughout the next year, Sasha was invited to over a dozen more parties. "It all started with beer." The teenage experimentation would escalate to marijuana and eventually hydrocodone. "My parents had warned me about bad friends. But these were good kids from good families." Within two years, Sasha tried oxycodone and harder drugs. Her grades spiraled, and she started skipping school to spend time with her new friends.

Her Mom's constant screaming reminded her that she had become a disappointment, a nuisance in her eyes. "The drugs helped to numb the pain," she remembered. At seventeen, she ran away for the very first time. It was a desperate cry for help that ended with her boyfriend hitting her: "I remember crying while he hit me." As she wept on the ground, bleeding and bruised, she begged him to stop. Afterward, the drugs continued to numb the physical pain while fueling the nightmare. Her tears became a constant companion.

Sasha's Mom would also shed tears over her future. It happened when Sasha ran away from home. It happened when she came back with bruises on her body. It happened when her Mom realized she had been lured into human trafficking by her so-called devoted boyfriend. It happened every time she saw her daughter.

She never imagined this nightmare would occur in their own lives. Sasha's heartbreaking story is sadly more common than people may realize. In the United States alone over half a million children run away from home every year. A third of them are lured in human trafficking within 48 hours of leaving their front door.[125] That means every month over 12,000 girls find themselves *in the same fate as Sasha*, living in red light districts where they are exploited and abused over and over again with African American girls disproportionally impacted by this serious problem.

The longer a girl remains on the streets or with friends, the greater the chance she will be swept into prostitution. In America, sex trafficking occurs whenever a person is forced or coerced into prostitution. Sasha, like thousands of girls before her, didn't stand a chance. Traffickers prey on the vulnerable. Many run away from home as a cry for help. In a crushing blow, the cry for help turns into a different nightmare.

Up to four million women and children are trafficked or lured across national and international borders for illegal sexual or labor purposes every year, according to the United Nations. Some victims are in plain sight, interacting with members of society, while others lead hidden lives in brothels, sweatshops, massage parlors, and even private homes. Adding to this problem is the lack of awareness, which leads to low victim identification. Only a fraction of these cases are brought to justice. Only a fraction of these victims find their way home again.

As she shares her story over a decade later, Sasha's tone remains detached and flat, as if she's emotionally withdrawn from the past. When asked about this detachment, she answers without hesitation, "It's how I survive."

Within the next decade, Sasha would be arrested twenty-six times for prostitution. What the police didn't know was that her blonde hair blued eyed boyfriend was forcing her to sell her body, even after a brutal rape. His reaction to her rape was to beat her for not bringing any money home. "I fell to the floor sobbing. This is how I lived my life. I was living in hell with this man."

## The Long Road Home

"The things I wanted in life weren't fancy," Sasha shared. "I just wanted a good man to love me." In the beginning, she believed she had found that. When she first met her "boyfriend," he showered her with compliments and bought her thoughtful gifts to show his love. Six months into the relationship, it took a violent turn. "That's when he started beating me to make money."

"It wasn't my dream to walk the streets," she said. "No one dreams of growing up and becoming a convicted felon."

Yet the same label that made her cringe would also become her saving grace.

In 2011, she was arrested for prostitution for the last time. Four days after her arrest, her "boyfriend" was also arrested for his role. Instead of being sent to prison because of her criminal history, Sasha had the good fortune of ending up in front of a groundbreaking mental health court in Chicago. The judge had witnessed the problem many times and ordered Sasha into drug treatment instead of prison. That was her saving grace. The combination of entering drug treatment and freedom from her boyfriend meant the possibility of a different life. Up until that day, she felt completely trapped in a life she had no control or hope in.

In treatment Sasha learned life-changing lessons. She learned that her painful past didn't define her future. She learned that an illness called addiction was ruining her life. She learned that it wasn't all her fault.

She learned that faith could help heal some of the emotional wounds that added to an already haunting existence. More importantly, she learned to forgive herself for allowing drugs to overtake her life. "That was the hardest lesson of all," she shared. "I should have known better."

Treatment taught Sasha that she could be her own worst enemy or best friend, and that even one drink or drug would send her back to a lifestyle that would definitely kill her. She also made the connection between bad choices, bad friends, and lost dreams. "There are consequences to every action— good or bad—I just never made that connection until later."

"I wish I could go back and talk to my fifteen-year-old self. There are so many things I would tell her. 'You are valuable as you are. You don't need other people's validation to be whole. You are enough. I just didn't realize it then. I didn't realize it for a long time."

In rehab, Sasha learned that her past could not be erased no matter how hard she tried, but her future was wide open. To help others avoid the same pain, she began telling her story in public. It was a difficult decision that became empowering after she joined forces with other victims. The experience changed her life. "Our purpose is to help prevent a new generation of victims. We know what they go through every day. It's not a life anybody dreams of."

"People forget that these women were all once innocent little girls with dreams. Instead they are mistreated over and over again." Rachel Ramirez, an organizer with the Chicago Coalition for the Homeless, agrees wholeheartedly and adds that a change in perception of sex-trafficking victims is essential in reversing the problem of human trafficking, a modern-day form of slavery, in the United States and around the world.[126]

It is estimated that two-thirds of those lured into sex trafficking in America are U.S. born like Sasha, while one-third are foreign-born women brought into this country under the deception of a better life, often with the lie of a job and a promising future. This problem is so widespread that it has been identified in all fifty states and the nation's capital.[127] This tragedy occurs in both large metropolitan areas to small rural towns. "These women are not criminals. The sooner we realize it, the better," Ramirez explained.

Some people believe that all women who become prostitutes and end up at large-scale sporting events like the Super Bowl are there because of their own doing, but that's not the entire story. "I would never want anyone to go through what I experienced. He owned me. I was like a piece of property. He made it clear that if I ever left, he would kill me," she shared as she looked away.

While Sasha talks about those stolen years, she realizes something unexpected. Where she had lost hope, she found renewed strength again, and it all came from the most unexpected of places—her painful and haunting past.

Sasha suddenly smiles as she talks about her future. She still dreams of her wedding day, but now her dreams include preventing a new generation of girls from going down the same path that almost killed her. "It all started out so innocently. I had no idea where it could go," she says. "That's the message people need to understand." As she ends her story, she explains that if one life is saved by sharing her journey, then there's proof that something positive can come from even the most painful of pasts. "Nothing is impossible," she says with a smile. "Not even that little girl's dreams."

Yet her story raises difficult questions that have been ignored for far too long. Specifically, how can this be stopped? How can we protect these children? And what happens when we, as consumers, support events that help make human trafficking a lucrative enterprise? Do the organizations running these events have an ethical obligation *to do anything at all*? Should we all just look the other way even though these are children being exploited in the worse way?

If the answer is no, then what can we do? What can the National Football League do? And can people like Sasha provide us access to a hidden, underground world that desperately needs our attention?

CHAPTER NINE

# THE WORLD CUP AND MODERN-DAY SLAVERY

While the Super Bowl is considered to be the single largest human trafficking event in the United States, there are widely reported concerns the World Cup is its equivalent on the global stage.[128] In the year before the 2014 World Cup games in Brazil, girls from the poorest areas of the country began to disappear.[129] Some ran away, like Sasha, while many were kidnapped right off the street. Some of the girls were as young as ten.[130] Their disappearance became national news, and at one point was such a problem that the police claimed "to have lost count" of the number of girls who went missing.[131]

The anti-trafficking and non-profit communities linked the mass disappearances to the upcoming World Cup games. The Vatican even spearheaded a campaign against human trafficking at the World Cup in Brazil.[132] Nuns camped outside the stadium, sharing flyers about child sexual exploitation and enslavement.

"Many of the young women were kidnapped from the slums of Brazil by sex traffickers and taken to the FIFA World Cup sites where they were used to service the construction workers building the soccer stadiums" and later the spectators during the games.[133]

Yet this wasn't the first time red flags had been raised. According to CBS News, "The risk of child exploitation increased by 30 to 40 percent during the World Cup in Germany in 2006 and South Africa in 2010."[134] It was reported that in "South Africa during the 2010 World Cup, estimates indicated about 100,000 people might have fallen prey to the schemes of traffickers."[135]

Advocates argued that some women and children were lured into the underground world of trafficking with false promises of jobs as tour guides, waitresses, or hotel employees, while others were coerced or taken against their will.

Behind the glamour of the World Cup games, the large stadiums, and the prestigious award, secrets were dying to come out. Those secrets threatened FIFA (Fédération Internationale de Football Association), the governing association for soccer, which oversees the World Cup. Yet most people would never guess that sex trafficking and labor trafficking could be a part of those potentially damaging secrets waiting to come out.

FIFA has continued to deny any and all claims and admits no wrongdoing in association with any activities that happen before, during, or after the World Cup. They claim that if any abuses occur, it is a small fraction and the governing body has done everything it can to stop these allegations.

In 2015, the new bribery scandal that rocked FIFA was only one of the potentially damaging shock waves coming out of the World Cup. The criminal charges mounted against sixteen FIFA officials by the U.S. Department of Justice included fraud, racketeering, money laundering, and bribery. U.S. federal prosecutors alleged that the defendants were part of a wide-reaching scheme that spanned twenty-four years to illegally gain money "through the corruption of international soccer."[136]

In the midst of these crushing international controversies, FIFA still bore the tremendous responsibility of organizing, overseeing, and executing the upcoming World Cup games every four years. The job of picking a new host city would be a global race against time, taking officials around the world.

Yet when the small Middle Eastern city of Doha in the country of Qatar was chosen among other, larger contenders to host the 2022 World Cup games, it came as a surprise to many in the international community. The city didn't have the infrastructure to host such a large-scale event given its size.

In preparation for the World Cup, freeways, hotels, stadiums, roads, a metro system, and even a new airport would need to be built from the ground up just to accommodate the swarm of people who would descend into Doha for the most highly anticipated and watched soccer game in four years.

Yet another controversy was building in the horizon. Critics and human rights activists became concerned that the accelerated speed needed to build Qatar into a modern-day global city had potentially led to some of the worst human rights abuses and allegations coming out of the Middle East.

In 2013, Amnesty International, an international human rights group, began a series of investigations into the alleged human rights abuses, sex and labor trafficking stories coming out of Qatar in preparation for the World Cup.[137]

Human rights activists and the media would ultimately report on two very different versions of Qatar.[138] One where wealth and glamour were on full display for millionaires and globe-trotting jet-setters to enjoy, and another highly different version of the country where some foreign workers were forced to surrender their passports (and essentially their freedom) to work for meager wages under horrendous living conditions.[139]

Two completely different stories were coming out of Qatar, which raised the most obvious and important questions: Which Qatar really existed? And how did the two very different narratives play into the scandal of the World Cup and modern-day slavery?

While millions of die-hard sports fans were focused on the upcoming games, others were studying the anomaly that was Qatar. Unlike any nation in the world, Qatar had the highest ratio of foreigners to citizens. Out of a population of over 1.7 million, only 225,000 people were actually citizens and lifetime residents of Qatar.[140] For every one citizen, there were over seven foreigners living in Qatar at any given time. Given this desperate need for foreign work, some envisioned a country that would pay high wages and have liberal immigration laws to support the growth and expansion of its framework.

Yet even with its high dependence and need for foreign workers, Qatar still had some of the most restrictive and limiting immigration laws in the Middle East.[141] These restrictions left foreign workers vulnerable to labor exploitation and even human trafficking, according to the Human Rights Watch.[142]

Up to 94 percent of Qatar's workforce comprised foreign workers ushered into the country to build specific projects, such as stadiums and hotels in anticipation for events like the

World Cup; statistically, that meant twenty new foreigners entered into the small country every hour, on a rotating basis.[143]

For some of these workers, the Kafala system would come to rule over their lives, literally and figuratively. The Kafala system has been equated to modern-day slavery by leaders such as Sharan Burrow, head of the International Trade Union Confederation.[144] Under its rules, workers had no choice but to surrender their passports to their employers, thereby limiting their movement and prohibiting their ability to leave the country without prior permission from their bosses. This requirement, along with meager pay and horrendous living conditions, appalled human rights advocates.[145]

Yet the issue wasn't money, since over $200 billion dollars was being devoted to build stadiums, freeways, hotels, apartments, and even public transportation in preparation for the 2022 World Cup. Given those figures, why were some workers paid low wages for their backbreaking physical work?

It was not just foreign workers who faced hostile conditions. Journalists attempting to report on the World Cup preparations in Qatar had been detained, arrested, and held while their equipment was seized and erased. The message was clear: when in Qatar, only report on what the government lets you see. Any "independent" reporting was seen as a threat to national security, and detention was not only possible but likely.[146]

In May 2015, a team from the BBC learned this firsthand while driving to film workers from Nepal. Eight unidentified cars forced the van carrying BBC journalists off the road. The journalists were arrested and detained in jail for two nights for failing to abide by the organized press tour. They had made the unfortunate decision of attempting to go outside the press tour to film a group of workers for independent reporting. This was treated as a national security threat, even though the reporters were later released and surprisingly asked to rejoin the preplanned press tour. Government officials acted as if nothing had happened. Not surprisingly, the BBC reporters returned home to England and wrote more about their detention than the organized press tour.[147]

While the team from BBC failed to gain access outside of the world the government had preauthorized for them to see, a team from ABC News had more luck. Unknown to the Qatar government, Greg Wilesmith and Eric Campbell began filming in a housing facility outside Doha, while Sharan Burrow pointed out a different world than what the government was portraying in their press tours. As they walked through a well-lit hallway in a published video, Burrow turned to the reporter and said, "You can see that on the outside this looks almost human. Then you walk in here and you see there are 300 men here in about 20 rooms."[148] In another clip, she says that they cook meals and wash "right next to the sanitation block" as the camera shows the footage.[149]

These reporters and advocate were not caught by the government. If they had been followed like the BBC journalists, detention and arrest would have been practically guaranteed. The ABC video was broadcast around the world and showed the squalor and filthy living conditions some workers lived under.

Any and all claims of subpar living conditions for World Cup workers have been vehemently denied by the government of Qatar. FIFA denied that World Cup workers lived in these kinds of conditions. They argued this represented a small fraction that was unknown to FIFA. They also denied the accusations that workers have died on job sites because of the unrelenting heat and dehydration.

When the *Washington Post* claimed that as many as 1,200 foreign workers had died while working on projects in support of the upcoming World Cup in Qatar and that as many as 4,000 were expected to die while creating the stadiums, highways, hotels, and other projects for the games, officials in the Qatar government shot back quickly with a rebuttal: "After almost five million work-hours on World Cup construction sites, not a single worker's life has been lost. Not one," the Qatari Government Communications Office responded.[150]

The *Washington Post* replied back by saying it "should have made clearer that the figures involved all migrant deaths in Qatar. A report by Qatar's government found 964 deaths of migrants from India, Nepal and Bangladesh in 2012 and 2013."[151]

Tragically, the controversy over dead foreign workers was not the only problem swirling around the World Cup like an uncontrollable tornado. The increase in child sexual exploitation was the next storm on the horizon. It is common knowledge among the anti-trafficking community that any national or international sporting event faces the same problem of child sex trafficking. What can be done to prevent this? Do we, as consumers, have a say in how our hard-earned money is spent supporting these global events? Are we as helpless as the girls who are kidnapped and sold into slavery when it comes to stopping or ending this? And if not, what message does our continued silence actually send?

With the increase in child trafficking during the World Cup, why hasn't FIFA, the international soccer association hosting the World Cup, put its anti-trafficking measures and campaigns into overdrive? What would it take for that to happen? In other words, how many more lives need to be exploited, and at what price?

CHAPTER TEN

# THE OLYMPICS AND HUMAN TRAFFICKING

Since the birth of the first modern Olympics in Athens, the games have continued to create a sense of awe and wonder. Known as the absolute pinnacle of athletic accomplishment, the Olympics are a global celebration of human potential and prowess at its very finest—an event athletes prepare their entire lives for.

To become an Olympian is to achieve something so rare and special that only a few are invited into its most exclusive club. The games are where heroes are born and dreams are achieved. The world is literally watching.

It's no wonder that hosting the Olympics can be just as prestigious. The process of picking a host city begins a decade before the opening ceremonies are ever unveiled. The process can take up to three years. The sustainability and legacy of each potential host city is examined for the coveted games. A long, detailed description reveals the extensive and time-consuming process for becoming an Olympic host city, but nowhere in the process are human rights ever mentioned.[152] They seem to be an afterthought in an activity that takes officials around the world with the purpose of choosing the "best" city for the historic games.

Yet some of the International Olympic Committee's (IOC's) selections for host cities have been controversial at best and scandalous at worse. The 2002 Olympic Games in Salt Lake City had one of the largest modern-day scandals in Olympic history, after accusations of bribery, money laundering, and backroom deals thrust the whole bidding process into the international spotlight.[153]

As a result of the fallout, ten members of the IOC were expelled or resigned in connection to the scandal.[154] The IOC initiated travel bans on all of its members. Members were forbidden from visiting any potential host cities on their own.[155] The only exception was when they were part of an official group sent under the watchful eye of the IOC.

Yet even with these unprecedented changes across the board, some were surprised when the 2014 Winter Olympics was awarded to the sleepy coastal town of Sochi, Russia. Sochi was known as the Russian Riviera, a small resort town for Russian leaders and the elite one-percent, making it an odd choice to host the Olympic Games, given its size and lack of basic infrastructure to hold such an event.

Once the decision was announced in 2007 that Sochi would host the Olympics, a rapid and unprecedented construction overhaul was put into place to convert the resort town into an international hub worthy of Olympic glory. Sochi would become a global city, overhauled by years of construction. Yet how would this unprecedented expansion take place, and who would provide the backbone for the unparalleled growth?

The conversion of Sochi from a quiet Black Sea resort community into an Olympic host city would become known as the largest construction project in Russian history.[156] In the frenzy to transform Sochi, the Olympic Committee would face some of its harshest allegations to date. And this time they were not based on the actual bidding process but on human rights and the hidden world of human trafficking.

The million-dollar question was whether Sochi could go from a relatively small vacation town to an international hub within seven years without any controversy or problems. And if not, who would pay the ultimate price?

No one knew exactly what to expect when researchers from an international human rights group, Human Rights Watch, descended upon Sochi. Rumors of modern-day slavery and other human rights injustices were swirling around the Russian Riviera like a tornado. The IOC and the Russian government denied any and all claims. The purpose of the researchers was to discover whether the connection of human trafficking to the Sochi Olympics was just an urban myth or whether the rampant rumors were a sign of deeper social problems lurking behind the almost $50 billion dollar expansion.

This was going to be the most expensive Olympics in history. Were the financial resources trickling down to the laborers who provided the backbone for this unprecedented growth? Would force labor tarnish this Olympics, or would the IOC be proud of what was uncovered in Sochi?

An investigation by Human Rights Watch revealed what human rights advocates feared the most.[157] Their investigation highlighted serious hidden problems behind some Olympic job sites. To transform Sochi, tens of thousands of workers were brought in from surrounding countries.[158] Workers migrated to Sochi from Ukraine, Armenia, Serbia, Moldova, and other nations.[159] The need for cheap labor was immediate and the opportunity for abuse a serious problem.

Workers interviewed by Human Rights Watch revealed hazardous working conditions and inadequate housing and food options.[160] Some reported the denial of full wages or delay in payment of earned wages and the inability for some to even leave the country.[161] Incidents of employers confiscating passports and failing to provide an employment contract were some of the damaging allegations in the widely circulated human rights report.[162] Some workers felt trapped in a system they had little power or control in.

Serious concerns were raised that Sochi would have an explosion of human trafficking not only during the actual games (similar to other large sporting events) but also sex and labor trafficking in the years of construction leading up to the games.

A typical human trafficking case had three distinct stages: (1) the recruitment of a person from one location (in the case of the Olympics, a neighboring country), (2) their transfer through a transit nation, and (3) the exploitation of that person in the destination city through either labor or sexual acts.[163]

The Olympics in Sochi had a surge of labor and sex trafficking before the opening ceremonies ever began. And even though the media was able to report on only a tiny fraction of what likely occurred, the stories were as shocking as the crime itself.

Reports of hundreds killed while working on Olympic sites leaked out of Sochi.[164] The exact numbers were impossible to pinpoint since methods for confirming such deaths remain elusive to outsiders and the Russian government and the IOC deny any deaths have occurred. Both the IOC and the Russian government have admitted no wrongdoing and are innocent under the law. Yet the denials give little comfort for the families who lost loved ones.


## SECRET DEATHS

Before the summer of 2013, newlyweds Mihai and his wife, Mariana, were on cloud nine after recently getting married and expecting a baby boy on the way. Like most couples in their early twenties, they worried about money, especially since well-paying jobs were dim in the struggling, ex-Soviet Republic of Moldova, where they lived. They hadn't won the birth lottery of being born in America or into a rich Soviet family with extensive connections. They were a young couple looking for the ability to support themselves.

When a friend told Mihai about well-paying jobs on Olympic sites over seven hundred miles away in Sochi, it seemed too good to be true. The pay at Olympic sites was reportedly five times greater than the average salary in Moldova. The idea of earning €1,000 per month (approximately $1,200 U.S. dollars) meant the young couple could begin their future on solid footing.[165]

Sadly, this story does not have the happy ending reserved for Hollywood movies. Mihai wouldn't live long enough to see the birth of his only son. Mariana would become a widow before her married life ever really began. And the mystery and questions surrounding his death would linger on long after his body was returned home unceremoniously in a casket.[166]

Mihai didn't die in battle. He didn't have the glory of dying for his beliefs or even standing up for his own basic rights. He died because contractors on a dangerous Olympic site saw the opportunity to exploit cheap labor. He had come with the hope of gaining employment to secure a better future for his family, but according to his cousin, Mihai died after being electrocuted while working on an Olympic job site. They were placing cables across fences on the perimeter without any proper training or safety precautions. A live cable hung low, and no one saw the accident, but by all accounts, the electricity should have been off. When Mihai's head touched the cable, he was electrocuted and died on impact.[167]

Even though there was a police investigation, Mariana would never get all the answers surrounding his death. Instead, his death certificate would state that Mihai was "unemployed," even though he was electrocuted while working on a job site.

The rest of the story sounds like a plot out of a James Bond movie. An unknown entity would pay for Mihai's body to be flown back to Moldova. At the Sochi airport, an unidentified man would approach Mariana with an envelope filled with cash for his funeral. Mihai's death and even his existence would be denied by those involved with overseeing the construction of the Olympic Games. According to contractors associated with the games, Mihai never really existed or died in Sochi. The only proof of his story would be his young widow's heartbreaking account and the birth of a child who would never know his father.

Was Mihai's story just one example of thousands of others who were silenced or died while working on Sochi Olympic sites? Or was his death just a random accident? The true number of those who lost their lives while working on Olympic sites is unknown. And when the head of an organization in Moscow published details and research regarding the deaths of migrant workers in Russia, instead of sparking further investigation or inquiry, *he was jailed for two months and then exiled from his country*.[168] His findings, along with those of two other Russian colleagues, claimed that almost "18,000 [migrants] died on Russian construction sites."[169]

The true number may always remain a mystery, but it could be argued that this was just another example of why the U.S. State Department listed Russia as a tier 3 country, meaning that the Russian government had not complied with even the minimal standards to combat human trafficking.[170]

As early as 2009, Human Rights Watch had warned the public and officials via documented reports of mistreatment of workers and made a call to action for the Russian government and the IOC to become more involved in overseeing the alleged human rights problems and curbing abuses.[171]

The issue became whether a portion of the $50 billion Olympic budget was being spent on giving *all* workers a fair salary with adequate housing, food, and protections for safety while fulfilling basic human rights. The concerns from Human Rights Watch were not based on just a few stories coming out of Sochi. Researchers interviewed sixty-six different workers who were working or had been working on Olympic sites in Sochi.[172] The stories coming out of actual work sites were disheartening and showed a pattern of abuse, from excessive working hours to little time off and failure to pay wages in part or in whole.[173]

Yet critics contended that the report was based on *only* sixty-six interviews, which raised the question, Was the sample size too small to reflect what was happening in Sochi? And if these abuses were examples of rare instances, why was the same pattern already witnessed in the construction leading up to the *Beijing* Olympics?[174] Was this déjà vu all over again, or was there a real, systemic problem with the IOC and its failure to even look into the history of human rights allegations of a country when picking potential host countries for a global event that sought to build a "peaceful and better world through educating youth through sport" and universal basic ethical principles?[175]

Should the IOC have a responsibility before, during, and after the Olympic Games to monitor human rights abuses directly with a task force or other government body with oversight power? Were the stories coming out of Sochi and Beijing mere coincidences or instances of forced labor coming out of the most celebrated event on Earth? If the human rights abuses had merit, should the world have boycotted the Olympics, or was the IOC ill prepared to deal with the reality of picking a host city with documented human rights abuses before the games even started?

After the allegations of abuse became public, the Russian government launched its own internal investigation. Russia's Deputy Prime Minister at the time, Dmitry Kozak, pledged that 277 million rubles (the equivalent of over $8 million U.S. dollars) would be paid for wages illegally withheld from those who had worked on Olympic sites.[176]

Human Rights Watch offered a stern warning to the IOC regarding forced labor, slave labor, and the future of the Olympics:

> The lesson from Sochi and the 2008 Beijing Olympics, where similar abuses occurred, is that awarding the Olympic Games to a country with a poor record on human rights and rule of law carries a strong risk that Olympic preparations will be a source of serious human rights abuses.
>
> To prevent further abuses, Human Rights Watch proposed concrete human rights reforms to the Olympic Charter, as well as requirements for the IOC to write human rights guarantees into the Host City Contracts and monitor implementation of those guarantees.[177]

The concern was whether the IOC had pushed the host governments to guarantee compliance with fair wages and universal human rights. "They simply take their word for it, and just act as bystanders," said Jane Buchanan, Associate Europe and Central Asia Director at Human Rights Watch, referring to human rights oversight by the IOC on Olympic construction sites.[178]

Will the Olympic Committee accept this international call to action to live up to their ideals? Will they rise to the occasion and become leaders in the fight against modern-day injustice and slavery? If not, then what will it take to make the

Olympics an event that shuns the worst forms of slavery and social injustice before, during, and after the games?

Only once the IOC put pressure on the host nation did any change occur. Had the IOC and the host government been monitoring the human rights problem from the very beginning, the stories coming out of Sochi could have been very different and actually lived up to the Olympic purpose of building a peaceful world through sportsmanship and respect for universal and ethical ideals.[179]

# PART III:

# SOLUTIONS

"What we have done for ourselves
alone dies with us.
What we have done for others and the world
remains and is immortal."

—Albert Pike

# CHAPTER ELEVEN

# SOLUTIONS TO A GLOBAL EPIDEMIC

*We are either a part of the problem or part of the solution.*
*We can light a candle to ignite change or allow this problem to grow in the dark.*
*It is ultimately up to each of us.*

I n history, every change first started as a thought, an idea that emerged greater than any one person or time. These visions for a different and better future benefited not only current generations but future generations yet to come. From the American Revolution to the Civil Rights Movement, and Black Lives Matter these shifts in consciousness and concerted action forward propelled society into another direction as new generation of leaders found their voice in a world that so desperately needed them.

Real change never grows in silence. It doesn't flourish behind closed doors in hushed voices with people who want to remain anonymous. It happens in public and start as seeds of chatter in chat rooms, boardrooms, and even classrooms. The

Red Movement is no different. These issues must be dealt with head on with the loudest voices possible.

Our only chance to fight modern-day slavery, social injustice, racism, discrimination, and the destruction of our environment is to open the doors of secrecy and misinformation to such epic proportions that no politician, person, or even corporation can ignore it ever again. Black Lives Matter opened people's eyes to the injustices in plain sight. Yet, what about the injustices that we don't see? What is our responsibility toward those?

Once these stories are out in the open, we have a chance to combat these problems. In the dark they will continue to increase and ruin a new generation of lives not yet born.

It starts with each of us. Each buying decision we make has greater consequences. Each choice has ramifications across the world. Buying cheap clothing by workers who are denied a livable wage sends a message to businesses that securing slave labor or forced labor to cut costs is somehow acceptable as long as the items are "at the right price." Supporting corporations who are destroying the environment sends the same message. Until we prioritize where our hard-earned money goes and begin to shop differently, nothing will change. It will only get worse.

As a collective group, we have enormous power to send a message around the world regarding the importance of private and public accountability, transparency in supply chains and the use of ethical labor practices to protect people and the environment.

We either help in destroying the environment and hurting people or we help save it, every single day, with every choice we make. It comes down to us. Just as we have inadvertently helped it grow with unchecked or unconscious consumerism, we can eradicate it with conscious consumerism that supports companies and events that forbid any kind of unethical labor practices or actions that harm the planet or people. These ideas must grow around the world and emerge greater than any one person, time, or country.

Listed below are ways modern consumers can start this fight. In no way is this list exhaustive. It is the beginning of a new chapter on fighting social injustice.

## Mobile Apps Fighting Modern-Day Slavery

Just as modern technology and outsourcing helped modern-day slavery flourish, it can also be a part of the solution to end it. Discovering whether the products you are purchasing are free of child labor, slave labor, or forced labor can be right at your fingertips.

Apps such as **Good On You** (ethical shopping app), **Good Guide**, the **Good Shopping Guide**, and **Ethical Barcode** make it easier for consumers to buy products knowing they are not supporting companies with unethical or illegal labor practices.

**Good On You** is a great source for finding trusted brands with ethical and environmentally sustainable fashion. The app allows shoppers to check the ratings on more than two thousand fashion brands while they shop.

**Greenstr—Consume Sustainably** is an innovative app that allows users to shop sustainably. By allowing your smartphone to become a scanner, it can scan barcodes and then provide ratings and other information to help shoppers be conscious consumers. This app lets people share their findings with family and friends while setting their ethical preferences from low to high in three different areas: social, ecological, and economical.

**HowGood** allows consumers to search or scan barcodes to quickly access a database of over two hundred thousand product ratings. The ratings show how environmentally friendly, minimally processed, and ethically produced the items are.

**Chocolate List** is another innovative app. It brings together research on companies that make vegan chocolate products to find out if their chocolate comes from areas where slavery occurs. Refusing to buy chocolate or coffee from areas where slavery is prevalent is a step toward eradicating this crime.

**Slavery Footprint** is another app that asks about your lifestyle choices, the clothes you wear, your eating habits, and your electronic use to determine how many slaves have contributed to your lifestyle. The interactive app shows all the different ways slave labor plays a role in our lives and provides an actual footprint of where our money is going.

Consumers can even send messages to their favorite brands, requesting them to address forced labor, child labor, and slave labor in their supply chains, through the app **Made in a Free World.**

Apps created to *fight sex trafficking* are also at our fingertips thanks to the miracle of modern-day technology. **Redlight Traffic** is a resourceful app that allows the public to report signs of human trafficking directly to the authorities related to a person, business, or a vehicle that shows suspicious behavior. This app allows the public to take pictures and provides education by sharing the red flags to look for when you suspect someone is a victim of sex trafficking.

According to **Redlight Traffic**, these are the warning signs: if the victim

- is injured or shows other signs of physical abuse,

- looks malnourished,

- has branding (tattoos) on the neck or lower back,

- always wears the same clothes regardless of the weather or circumstances, or

- has few personal possessions.

This app also educates consumers about victim behavior. A victim may:

- -be disoriented and not know where he or she is;

- act fearful, nervous, passive, tense, paranoid, or subservient;

- avoid eye contact and appear hesitant to talk to strangers; or

- seem to have rehearsed responses in social interactions.

- Information Courtesy of **Redlight Traffic**

**The STOP APP** also allows the public to report incidents and upload pictures and videos to fight sex trafficking. It shares the signs to look for and allows users to anonymously report behavior. This was created by www.stopthetraffik.org.

Another creative app to fight sex trafficking is **TraffickCam**. This app was designed for anyone who travels regularly and comes across suspicious behavior. The app allows the public to take pictures of hotel rooms (where victims of trafficking are often found) and upload them to **TraffickCam's** database. This app has an 85 percent success rate because the pictures are analyzed and compared to a national database of pictures provided by the police.

Law enforcement agencies around the nation can cross-reference the hotel room pictures of trafficking victims that appear online to search for similarities and find the location of victims. With the user's location pinpointed, the authorities know exactly where to look. Search algorithms also provide the police with the most probable location of the victim to cut down on the time needed to intervene and rescue them. This app has the potential of revolutionizing the fight against human trafficking by involving the public in real-time investigations and increasing the ability of police to find victims.

The **Lifeboat ACT Game** and **BAN Human Trafficking!** apps help a new generation of activists learn about this crime along with how to protect themselves and their friends from becoming victims. By playing interactive games, the user learns of the different stages of trafficking from recruitment, deception, exploitation, and escape. This app is a must-have for teenagers.

The apps above, along with the following list, are using the modern miracle of technology to help eradicate modern-day slavery one-click at a time:

- **Trafficking Info.** This app provides a guide to help vulnerable, at-risk youth who are susceptible to child trafficking.

- **Sweat & Toil.** This app developed by the U.S. Department of Labor provides extensive information on the problems of child labor and forced labor around the world. It also provides a list of goods produced by child labor or forced labor and the countries those products are harvested from.

- **Run 2 Rescue Organization.** This app seeks to find, rescue, and help victims of sex trafficking in the United States. Users can help the fight by learning more about the issue, volunteering, or becoming a mentor or support home, as well as donating to the group.

- **SafeResponse.** This app allows people to donate essential items or services needed by victims of trafficking and victims of domestic violence. Donors can make donations right on the app, fulfilling the needs of victims in real time.

- **Project Rescue.** This organization works to help and rescue victims of slavery and is working with affiliated ministries in France, Spain, Finland, Bangladesh, Tajikistan, Moldova, Nepal, and India.

- **Sex Traff.** This app is designed by and for health care professionals to discern patients at risk for being sexually exploited and how to help them.

- **Awake VR.** This is an app that shares the stories of seven girls escaping the web of trafficking. It provides an insider look into the problem.

In no way is the list of apps above exhaustive, and as agents for change we encourage everyone to develop and find new apps that will fight all forms of slavery.

## SUPPORTING COMPANIES WITH ETHICAL AND TRANSPARENT SUPPLY CHAINS

New businesses are emerging every day with the mission to be ethically conscious and environmentally friendly. Numerous studies confirm that up to 70 percent of consumers under the age of thirty-five believe that choosing a brand or item based on ethical practices is important. And the market is responding to them.

Environmentalists and human rights activists praise new concepts such as clothes sharing for high-end pieces, such as Rent the Runway. This encourages shoppers to rent instead of buying and discarding high-end clothes after only wearing them a few times.

The now successful and high-profile apparel line Everlane was at first ridiculed by industry insiders when it initially opened and provided detailed information about its raw materials and factories to ensure ethical standards. Those early insiders thought consumers could care less about such minuscule things. They could not have been more wrong. Everlane is now a leader in the ethical-shopping industry and has grown tremendously since its early days, thanks to consumers who care about where their hard-earned money is going.

The following is a list of ethical, transparent companies and websites that should be on the shopping list of every conscious consumer who wants to fight modern-day slavery:

1.  **Compare Ethics**
    This company connects ethical shoppers to ethical brands online and in communities. The founders of this company strive to create a one-stop shop where brands who care about fair wages, the environment, and treatment of animals are easily accessible to consumers who want to find them.
    Shop at www.CompareEthics.com

2. **Everlane**

   Everlane believes that everyone can make a difference. They believe in radical transparency, ethical factories that provide fair wages, and exceptional quality in creating their products. This company is on the forefront of using consumerism to change the world one purchase and person at a time.

   Shop at www.Everlane.com

3. **Fashion Heroes**

   This website celebrates brands making a difference by highlighting various companies changing the world and their founders. It also provides in-depth information for consumers who want to educate themselves and learn more about how shopping choices can create rippling effects.

   Shop at www.FashionHeroes.cco

4. **TO THE MARKET**

   TO THE MARKET was created because its founder and CEO, Jane Mosbacher Morris, realized the demand by Millennials and Generation-Zs for ethically made products. She witnessed untapped talent around the world from artisans and women-owned businesses and realized they could fulfill the demand. TO THE MARKET is on a mission to change the way products are made to create a better future for people, the planet, and ultimately business that fosters the greater good for everyone involved and not just the top one percent.

   Shop at www.ToTheMarket.com

## 5. GoodWeave

For the last twenty-five years, GoodWeave has been a leader in using purchasing power to create change around the world by pioneering a market for products made without child labor by preventing and rescuing children from slavery. Goodweave's team of field inspectors and social workers verify that items purchased with the GoodWeave label are free of child trafficking and labor in all aspects of their supply chain. Their mission is to wipe out forced labor, child labor, and all forms of modern-day slavery through on-the-ground verification of factories making products with the GoodWeave label.
Shop at www.GoodWeave.org

## 6. Reformation

Reformation's website states that "being naked is the #1 most sustainable option. Reformation is #2." Their environmental consciousness, along with their mission to make sure workers get a fair wage, makes Reformation a leader in their industry. They sell a wide variety of clothing from wedding dresses to basic T-shirts. Their mission is to celebrate women while leaving behind a positive legacy.
Shop at www.TheReformation.com

## 7. Fair Indigo

Their website eloquently states that "when fashion is done right, we all do well. You, us, farmers, garment workers, and our shared home, Planet Earth." Their goal is to lift people up by providing a livable wage to workers and creating timeless pieces for every woman. Shop at www.FairIndigo.com

## 8. Fair Trade Winds

Their website states that "people and the planet should not be exploited for the things we buy." This company provide unique gifts with a purpose since all their products are handmade and verified by Fair Trade to give workers a fair, livable wage. This family-run business cares about families around the world and wants to give workers the opportunity to send their kids to school and build up communities while creating high-quality, ethically produced items for the public.
Shop at www.FairTradeWinds.net

## 9. Eileen Fisher

This company believes that social injustice is the reason to do business differently. Fair working conditions are the cornerstone of their business model and by 2020 their goal is to have a no-waste facility manufacturing their clothes. The inclusivity of various body sizes, from small to 3X, makes them a winner for women of all shapes and sizes who want to care for the world while remaining fashionable.
Shop at www.EileenFisher.com

## 10. Boden

Boden started off as a UK retailer and now has taken the world by storm. They have factories in seventeen

countries and are committed to fair rights and wages for workers and environmentally solid production and pieces. They sell clothing for babies, men, and women with a sense of style that is timeless.
Shop at www.Boden.com

## 11. Patagonia

If you are looking for stylish outdoor men's and women's clothing made by Fair Trade factories in India, Sri Lanka, and Los Angeles, then Patagonia is for you. They are also one of the first companies in activewear to use recycled material and organic cotton while expanding their commitment to ethical labor.
Shop at www.Patagonia.com

## 12. Monsoon

Based in London, this company provides special occasion apparel for the conscious consumer, from wedding dresses to flower girl dresses and shoes. This company provides one-of-a-kind pieces while protecting workers and the environment.
Shop at www.MonsoonLondon.com

## 13. ABLE

ABLE is a lifestyle brand with a purpose. Their goal is to end generational poverty by providing economic opportunities to women who may not experience them otherwise. While living in Ethiopia, the founder witnessed how extreme poverty trapped women, generation after generation, into prostitution as the only means for survival. Afterwards, ABLE was born with the goal is to end generational poverty one purchase and one job at a time.

Shop at www.LiveFashionable.com

## 14. Krochet Kids Intl.

This affordable line aims to change the world by empowering their artisans through fair wages, mentoring programs, and educational opportunities. They leave behind a positive impact in the communities that make their products, and their stories of change inspire a new generation of social activism in business.

Shop at www.KrochetKids.org

## 15. Armedangels

Armedangels believe that a fashion revolution is underway for the soul and future of fashion. They were inspired to ignite change after the Rana Plaza building collapsed killing 1,138 people. Many of the victims were poorly paid apparel workers who gave their lives in the pursuit of creating a better future for themselves and their families. After this tragedy, Armedangels was born, and they work with partners to ensure fair wages, working conditions, and environmental standards behind every garment they sell to create real change.

Shop at www.Armedangels.de

# BRANDS THAT CARE ABOUT THEIR ENVIRONMENTAL FOOTPRINT

The brands listed below care deeply about their environmental footprint and are a great list to add to your arsenal for shopping in an eco-conscious way. In no way is this list exhaustive, and you are encouraged to find or start your own brand that keeps environmental impact and/or workers' fair wages a top priority.

1. **Tentree**

   For every item purchased they plant ten trees. To date they have planted twenty-five million trees with the goal of planting one billion trees by 2030. (At this rate, we think they will surpass that goal.) Their mission is to inspire a new generation towards change. They sell women's and men's clothing, outerwear, and accessories. This ecofriendly company uses sustainable fabrics and practices that support the environment. Prices range from $34 (tank) to $130 (jacket).
   Shop at www.tentree.com

2. **Alternative Apparel**

   This company is a leader in ecofriendly clothing and also work with factories around the world that provide fair and safe working conditions for their workers. They use ecofriendly products, and their best-sellers are a must for every wardrobe. Their price range is $15 (tanks) to $150 (denims).
   Shop at www.alternativeapparel.com

3. **Amour Vert**

   To ensure all their pieces are ethically produced, all of their items are created within twenty miles of their San Francisco office. They use zero waste and dyes that are non-toxic for the environment. For each tree they use, they plant a new one, with over 130,000 trees planted to date (and growing). They sell items online and also have stores in Berkeley, San Francisco, Palo Alto, Newport Beach, and Santa Monica, California, along with Atlanta, Georgia, and Seattle, Washington. Price ranges from $48 (tanks) to $200 (dresses).
   Shop at www.amourvert.com

4. **Cienne**

   Cienne is a ready-to-wear collection for women who care about quality and ethically sourced fashion. Their mission is based on three principles: empowering people, producing items in a responsible manner, and preserving and increasing craftmanship. They design clothes in small batches to eliminate excess waste, with 100-percent natural dyes, and focus on unique designs that make pieces practically one of a kind. Prices range from $67 (scarfs) to $485 (jackets).
   Shop at www.ciennenewyork.com

5. **Cuyana**

   They create timeless, iconic pieces for modern women with attention to detail by skilled and well-paid crafts-men throughout the United States, Europe, and South America. Their mission is to empower women, and with each purchase they send customers a linen bag they can fill with used clothing that is donated to a women's organization helping victims of abuse start over in life. This company encourages women to buy fewer and higher quality items to decrease their environmental footprint on the earth.

Shop at www.cuyana.com

## 6. EcoVibe Apparel

They are known for their affordable and ethical fashion line. They focus on soft fabrics and items that are ethically produced, including jewelry and accessories that are made locally from natural and recycled items. EcoVibe also donates one percent of all their sales to a nonprofit named One Percent for the Planet to help protect the environment. Since its inception, One Percent for the Planet has helped distribute hundreds of millions of dollars to nonprofits focused on the environment around the world. Prices range from $29 (tanks) to $98 (dresses).

Shop at www.ecovibeapparel.com

## 7. Pact

Pact uses organic cotton for their clothes that consumes up to 95 percent less water than other cotton. To date, over fifty-one million gallons of water have been saved by Pact customers. They also avoid harsh chemicals to keep their clothes softer and more durable. They provide men's and women's underwear, tops, pants,

dresses, and loungewear. Their line is the most affordable with prices starting at $9 (T-shirts) to $40 (dresses).
Shop at www.wearpact.com

8. **People Tree**
This company combines the best of both worlds and has been a pioneer in sustainable fashion, starting their journey in 1991. They create clothes ethically by using living wages and Fair Trade, so the workers who make the clothes also benefit. Their clothes use dyes that are less harmful, ecofriendly materials, and organic products. Their labels are even made from paper that is harvested in a responsible manner. This company takes conservation to the next level. The price range is $15 (tops) to $200 (dresses).
Shop at www.peopletree.co.uk

9. **Threads 4 Thought**
This eco-conscious company helps the environment by using recycled, organic, and sustainably produced materials to create activewear, dresses, tops, pants, and accessories for men and women. The price range is $12 (tank tops) to $65 (hoodies).
Shop at www.threads4thought.com

For more ecofriendly products visit: www.onyalife.com/eco-friendly-products or www.onyalife.com

# Goods Made by Survivors of Human Trafficking or Other Vulnerable Groups

One of the best ways to fight human trafficking is to buy products made by former slaves who have escaped the web of trafficking and at-risk individuals who are able to escape by making a living creating handmade, often one-of-a-kind products. By supporting the following companies who employ them, the idea of shopping with a purpose takes on a whole new dimension.

1. **Freeset USA**

   Freeset was started in one of Asia's largest districts for sex trafficking. Some of the women were kidnapped from homes and communities. This company helps women return home to work in businesses and ensure their children are never trafficked.

   Shop at www.FreesetUSA.com

2. **Awaken Fair Trade**

   Their mission is to help end human trafficking by giving victims employment opportunities that allow them to break free. Their varied collection is made by women who have escaped trafficking, and their one-of-a-kind products have something for everyone, from scarves to bracelets to apparel and even home goods. Their goal to create a business that changes lives has helped them flourish, and in the process, survivors have too.

   Shop at www.AwakenFairTrade.com

3. **Rethreaded.com**

   Every purchase from Rethreaded gives freedom to women impacted by the sex trade. Through their Freedom Business Partners, four thousand women have gained employment and an opportunity to "renew hope, reignite dreams, and release potential for survivors of human trafficking locally and globally through business," according to their website. Their retail and online store offer products made by survivors that showcase their talent from around the world.

   Shop at www.ReThreaded.com

4. **BRANDED Collective**

   "Many victims of human trafficking are BRANDED; their captors physically mark them with a number or symbol. This process is often violent: a forced tattoo, a burn or knife cut. The BRANDED Collective stands against this brutal practice. Each BRANDED item is stamped with an initial and number. The initial belongs to the survivor who made your jewelry," according to their website.[180] And each survivor's story can be found on their website. As an added bonus, consumers can register the unique number and send messages of hope to the survivor of trafficking who made their piece.

   Shop at www.BrandedCollective.com

5. **War Chest Boutique**

   Their retail and online store provide a treasure chest of unique gifts made by at-risk and rescued men and

women from the slave trade. Every product purchased from War Chest Boutique comes with a card sharing the personal story of the person who made it. Their invitation to shop with a purpose inspires a new generation to use their shopping power for the greater good.
Shop at www.WarChestBoutique.com

6. **Trades of Hope**
This brand provides hope to both the people they employ and the consumers who buy their products. They have changed thousands of lives in sixteen countries by providing employment and opportunities. Each purchase helps a mom feed her family and send her children to school. Based in Florida, Trades of Hope works with thousands of artisans around the world to uplift people from poverty and create impactful jewelry and accessories that are unique and one-of-a-kind.
Shop at www.MyTradesofHope.com

7. **Starfish Project**
Each purchase from this innovative company supports rehabilitation and aftercare programs for survivors of trafficking through shelter, education, counseling, and employment. One hundred percent of the sales from their jewelry are reinvested into services to give survivors a new chance at life. Survivors learn job skills, and many eventually go on to become graphic designers, managers, photographers, and/or accountants. Their jewelry collection are conversation starters that help

spread awareness and make an impact to end human trafficking.

Shop at www.StarfishProject.com

## 8. Purpose Jewelry

This jewelry is made by victims of modern-day slavery. Every artisan is given education, employment, counseling, and medical care through their non-profit, International Sanctuary. They change lives one product at a time and wholeheartedly believe that style and making a difference can be integrated in a way that changes the lives of women who have endured the unthinkable.

Shop at www.PurposeJewelry.org

## 9. Sudara

This company sells unique pajamas, robes, and lounge pants made by women at risk or those who have survived slavery. They provide a living wage and skilled training to their employees and bold designs and bright colors to their consumers. Their various designs for menswear and even children's clothing make them a well-rounded company that also sells one-of-a-kind accessories for you and your favorite pet.

Shop at www.Sudara.org

## 10. Good Paper

This is an innovative company whose mission is to restore the human spirit. They employ women in India who have escaped sex trafficking by selling unique cards created by them and sold around the world.

Shop at www.GoodPaper.com

For more, visit www.InternationalHumansRights.com under the post "Brands Fighting Modern Day Slavery."

## Fair Trade Products and Third-Party Monitoring

History has shown that consumers who demand and even boycott companies who have unethical practices or policies that harm the environment are not only effective but create transformation by hitting companies where it hurts. One way to demand more is by asking companies to use Fair Trade certification in their business.

*Fair Trade certification* is a third-party monitoring system that shows fair labor standards have been met on farms that develop and produce coffee, chocolate, tea, and other everyday items. The certification also helps raise the income of farmers so they can pass the benefits on to their workers.

Buying Fair Trade coffee, chocolate, and other items works because it creates accountability and ensures a living wage, fair prices, and community benefits for the farmers and workers who make the products. Supporting and purchasing Fair-trade-certified products has shown to systematically decrease poverty while safeguarding ethical labor conditions and promoting environmentally sound methods in producing everyday products.

Another example is the GoodWeave certification. It is also a third-party monitoring system that guarantees that hand-made rugs created around the world are free of child labor. Yet these are only two examples. Consumers need to demand new and ongoing certification and monitoring programs so ethical shopping can become as prevalent and common as buying organic items. It needs to become the norm, not the exception, for modern-day slavery to end.

## Cooperatives That Create a Better Future

The growth of Fair Trade in fighting social injustice has led to the rebirth of cooperatives in third world countries. A cooperative is a group-based business that can form for economic and social good. They help create change in the way work is organized and wealth is distributed.

Cooperatives are member-owned, member-centered, and member-controlled. Ownership and control by members are a vital aspect in making cooperatives a tool in fighting poverty since it gives members a greater voice, which often means greater wages in the industry, and that increase is then transferred to the communities they live in.

Cooperatives can ensure their businesses and supply chains are free of child labor, slave labor, or forced labor. Cooperatives can help provide livable wages to their employees while providing leadership in communities to provide educational, medical, and basic social services.

The potential of cooperatives around the world is untapped and is vital in ending child labor, forced labor, and slave labor in the chocolate and coffee industries, two industries that desperately need to be reformed. By supporting cooperatives and companies that work with them, we give communities a chance to fight the problem of human trafficking in their own backyard.

Cooperatives are the future, and it's the consumer who can spearhead the transformation through informed consumerism driven by a global mission to do good. By helping farmers in developing countries escape poverty, cooperatives can share the financial benefits with the workers and the communities they all live in to end social injustice.

## Recycled and Reused Items Stop the Cycle

One of the most environmentally friendly ways to shop and decrease the slavery footprint is by buying used clothing, electronics, and everyday products. It helps keep items out of overfilled landfills that contaminate the environment.

Consignment stores, vintage stores, and antique stores are growing in towns across the world, taking old items and rebranding and reselling them to consumers who want to be environmentally and ethically conscious. This is an excellent way to protect the environment and limit a new generation of victims by taking what has been made and extending its shelf life.

This is especially true in the clothing industry, where in the United States less than 20 percent of clothes end up being donated or recycled every year. This means at least 80 percent end up in landfills (over ten million tons of clothing and garments end up in landfills *in the U.S. alone*). Globally the problem is even more of an environmental nightmare, with up to 20 percent of the harsh and harmful chemicals used to keep clothes a specific color ending up in bodies of water next to production centers in developing countries. These chemicals leave behind a harmful effect on the ecosystem and quality of these bodies of water, affecting all forms of marine life and spreading to other connected bodies of water.

Extending the life of a piece of clothing by even a year decreases the waste and water impact by up to 30 percent. Now imagine doing that for even just one ton of clothing. Then multiply that by millions of tons, and now we have impact that is so enormous and takes no more energy than deciding to donate your clothes to be resold locally or recycling the ones you already have instead of throwing them away.

During the Great Depression, it wasn't uncommon for people to keep clothes until they came back into style again many years later. We may now laugh at that notion, but the idea of keeping a garment and using it again even years or decades later is not just environmentally sound but economically impactful as well. Think about how much money you would save and how much of an environmental impact you could have by just keeping and wearing the clothes in your closet now and for the next ten years by buying classic pieces that never go out of style. That alone leaves a positive impact that is hard to comprehend on a global level.

Not only is recycling important, but the next ultimate step in protecting the environment is to design clothes that will decompose at the end of their lives, meaning they will disintegrate into the environment, leaving behind no toxicity. The environmental impact would be greatly beneficial for future generations and could help fashion get away from its notorious reputation of being the second-largest polluting industry in the world (behind oil and gas).

## Spread the Message for Social Change

There are so many ways to spread the message about how social injustice and our purchasing power can make rippling effects around the world. These are just a few ways to get you started:

1. Organize a social gathering or group to discuss the issues in person.

2. Host a letter-writing party to pressure your favorite brands to create ethical and transparent supply chains while promoting environmental safeguards.

3. Host a community event like a barbecue, block party, or movie screening about modern-day slavery to raise awareness and advocacy.

Here is a list of short films, documentaries, and movies to get you started:

> *Call + Response*
> *California's Forgotten Children*
> *China Blue*
> *The Corporation*
> *The Dark Secret Behind Your Favorite Makeup Products*

*Eden*
*The Dark Side of Chocolate*
*Food Chains*
*Human Trafficking*
*I Am Jane Doe*
*In Plain Sight*
*Not My Life*
*Stopping Traffic*
*The Storm Makers*
*Taken*
*This Is Human Trafficking: A WRAL.com Original Series*
*Trade of Innocents*
*Trafficked*
*Tricked*
*The True Cost*
*The Ugly Face of Beauty*
*Very Young Girls*

4. Make a Facebook page about the issues and invite your friends to join in, discuss, and ask questions.

5. Use Instagram, Snapchat, and WhatsApp to relay information about the Red Movement to your friends and family.

6. Talk to your neighbors and friends one-on-one about the issue of slave labor, child labor, and forced labor, and mobilize them on how they can help change the future.

7. Create a chapter in your community to fight human trafficking in all its forms and protect the environment by writing letters to CEOs of companies. By creating an army of volunteers to get the message out, this movement can have changing effects for generations to come.

8. Talk to your kids and encourage them to become ambassadors of freedom while they are still young.

9. Brainstorm ways your community, family, and friends can make a difference in the fight against human trafficking while protecting the environment.

10. Boycott brands that refuse to make fair wages, human rights, and protecting the environment a cornerstone or priority in their business model for the greater good.

11. Engage in *shareholder activism* by educating yourself on the labor and environmental practices of your favorite brands. By buying just one stock of a publicly traded company, you can push for and demand social change in that company. When you buy shares of publicly traded companies, you technically become a part owner because you own a part of the company. That gives you the right to attend and speak at the Annual General Meeting of the company you own (even one) stock in. At this meeting, you can ask questions of the board of directors on issues that are important to you. This gives consumers that chance to directly deal with the boards of companies that don't make human rights and

the environment a priority and to celebrate the ones that do.

We need to not only increase awareness but create a shift in thinking where businesses understand that consumers *will not support* harmful practices that hurt humans or the environment just so the companies can make a greater profit margin. Instead, consumers will support businesses that seek out ways to discover and stop exploitation in their supply chain while awarding leaders who take on the responsibility of eradicating human trafficking and protecting the environment. There has to be a shift in business, and it starts with the *consciousness of consumers who create that shift and leverage change.*

As consumers we have the right to demand that our favorite brands enact fair labor standards and environmental protections. This is for all industries, including but not limited to toy makers, electronics companies, and even companies that supply us with food.

If individuals break the law by exploiting another, there are consequences. Then why are corporations given a free pass? *We must outlaw corporate privilege by demanding the same consequences for organizations and companies as we do for all citizens.* There are no reasons international corporations should not have the same accountability. And not knowing whether slave labor, forced labor, or child labor exists in their supply chain is no excuse. Humans can't use ignorance as a defense when breaking the law. So why can corporations use it? It is the worst form of privilege, and it has been going on for far too long.

Laws need to be changed to reflect this. Companies make millions from products; therefore, it is their *responsibility* to know whether their workers are being exploited and whether their practices are harming the environment.

Megabrands like the National Football League in America, the Olympics, and the World Cup are no different. They make tens of millions of dollars from the sporting events they host. On a moral level, these brands have more of a social responsibility than just providing entertainment to their fans or supporters.

Consumers are the ones who support and ultimately help fund these sporting events. Because of their continued support, these brands have an ethical responsibility to make sure these events don't result in the destruction of young lives through any form of sex trafficking or labor trafficking. Everyone has a significant role in fighting modern-day slavery and social injustice.

E-V-E-R-Y-O-N-E

For any organization or league, whether national or international, to look the other way and ignore this serious problem should be a crime that not only creates a dark cloud over that brand but impacts its goodwill and global reputation while showing callous indifference to the very people who support them and the vulnerable people who are put in harm's way because of their events.

Why are individuals held to a higher standard than these organizations? Should it not be the other way around? For example, if parents of teenagers host a party and teenagers drink at that party and hurt others by drinking and driving, the parents can be held criminally and civilly accountable. So why do organizations get a free pass when negligence happens on their watch as well?

These organizations are hosting these events. They should not be held above the law, nor should they be allowed to look the other way. The Red Movement is about all entities, large and small, being held to the same standard. No one gets a free pass just because they are rich and influential. No. One.

Therefore, consumers can demand that their favorite sporting associations or leagues take an active role in fighting any type of modern-day slavery that happens on their watch be it labor trafficking or sex trafficking. The issue is not whether organizations have a responsibility. They have an ethical and moral responsibility.

The issue is why haven't these organizations already taken a stand to prohibit and stop this behavior and make it a part of their global mission to end all forms of exploitation that happens on their watch?

Monitoring abuses and exploitation at these global and national sporting events through a third party or new department, or even assisting law enforcement in stopping these crimes, supports these organizations' goal of working to make the world better through sports.

Yet the real work starts before a host country is even selected for the Olympics and the World Cup. These governing bodies should only consider host countries who have appropriate human trafficking and human rights laws, procedures, and policies in place. These games should not be given to countries with horrendous human rights abuses because it essentially gives those countries a stamp of approval.

And once a host city is selected, the Olympics and World Cup should work with them to develop an action plan to combat the increase of human trafficking linked to these games, be it through sex or labor trafficking.

These events are more than just sporting events. They are global celebrations bringing together the world's top athletes to show the best humanity has to offer. It's time these sporting events left a legacy everyone can be proud of and uphold the very values they were created upon.

It is long overdue.

# CHAPTER TWELVE

# NEW LEGAL AND SOCIAL FRAMEWORKS

*A man may die, nations may rise and fall, but an idea lives on.*
—*John F. Kennedy*

I t's no secret that international and domestic laws need to evolve over time to keep up with the changing needs of society.

Under the Thirteenth Amendment of the United States Constitution, it is illegal to hold any person in involuntary servitude through use of threats, force, or coercion that equals imprisonment.[181] Yet why does this **not** extend to corporations who use slave labor or forced labor to create products that are then sold here in the United States? These companies are violating the Constitution and *profiting from it here in the U.S.,* but they get a free pass because of the proximity of the crime and/or their privilege? The answer is an astonishing, yes.

To keep the legal framework "as is" and make no changes to laws to create public accountability and transparency would be an injustice that goes against the specific intent and purpose behind the Thirteenth Amendment. The reality is that slavery never ended, and laws have not progressed to stop it once and for all. Slavery just changed form, and our laws have inadvertently *helped it expand by not changing with the times to truly fight it.*

Up until now, millions of people have been unaware that companies overseas have been given a free pass for decades when it comes to using slave labor, even though their items are sold here, while individuals in the United States would be prosecuted for the *exact same crime and spend years or decades in prison* for using slave labor or forced labor to create and sell products in the United States.

As a society, we can do better. We must do better. Millions of people deserve a life free from this. It is up to us to create and inspire change across the board. Radical transparency in business is desperately needed for the spirit, intent, and purpose of the Thirteenth Amendment to be followed.

A new legal framework is essential on the state and federal levels that holds corporations in the United States and abroad liable for human rights violations both civilly and criminally when their *products end up on U.S. soil.* The fact that these products end up here should be enough to give U.S. courts jurisdiction (authority) to decide these cases. Yet the laws currently don't allow it. *This must change, and new laws need to reflect this shift, otherwise these companies will continue to have no accountability for their actions, and these problems will only grow as they have for decades.*

*It will continue to get worse.*

In addition to expanding the jurisdiction of U.S. courts for products sold here, new laws must demand transparency in business by adopting a strict liability model. Strict liability is a legal model in which intent does not have to be proven as an element of guilt. In other words, by adopting the strict liability model corporations cannot escape their responsibility by saying, "We did not know." For individuals, ignorance is not a legal defense when breaking the law, *so why should it be for corporations? Why are they given a free pass?*

Any corporation who has slave labor or forced labor in their supply chain or contributes to the destruction of the environment should *be held accountable through criminal and civil courts.* New laws must make corporations criminally and civilly liable for allowing these crimes to continue, *no matter where that occurs.*

These new laws need to reflect that since these products are sold in the United States, that gives U.S. courts jurisdiction (authority) to decide matters relevant to the Thirteenth Amendment of the Constitution and the degradation of the environment. Anything less supports the growth of modern-day slavery and environmental destruction by allowing it to grow without any real accountability.

Both the corporate entity as well as its highest-ranking officials need to be personally liable. This may seem radical at first, but it's the only way to guarantee real change, by making executives and business leaders accountable through fines and jail time; otherwise *these issues will never end.* They will just continue to grow as they have for decades.

On the state level, there has been small progress. In 2012, the California Supply Chain Transparency Act legally required large companies with over $100 million in revenue every year who do business in California to publicly disclose their anti-trafficking practices and policies (if any).[182] This law is a step in the right direction but still grossly inadequate, because it does not *force companies to stop violating the Thirteenth Amendment* and fight modern-day slavery through required auditing models and internal investigations to keep their supply chain free of slavery. Corporations can stop this problem or be criminally and civilly liable. That is what the new laws need to clearly state.

Federal bills similar to the California Supply Chain Transparency Act have stalled on the national level, showing what little progress our lawmakers have made. The Business Supply Chain Transparency Act introduced in 2011, 2014, 2015, and 2018 in the U.S. Congress has currently stalled once again for the fourth time.[183] This must change. This law would require businesses with over $100 million in global gross receipts to disclose actions taken to identify and address conditions of slavery in their supply chain. There is no legitimate reason these laws should stall in Congress. They need to be passed immediately and should be widened to apply to more corporations than just ones that gross over $100 million a year since there is a universal prohibition against slavery. The law should also force corporations to investigate their supply chains to make sure their workers are given a livable wage without violations to their basic human rights. Leaving it up to companies to regulate themselves has failed. That is where laws need to step in and create real consequences for change.

In addition, new laws need to be created that allow U.S. consumers to have standing (the ability) to sue overseas companies that violate the Thirteenth Amendment or contribute to the destruction of the environment when their products are sold here in the United States.

For example, the Alien Tort Statute must be explicitly expanded to include human rights violations here and abroad.

The Alien Tort Statute is a section of federal law that states, "The district courts shall have original jurisdiction of any civil action by an alien for a tort only, committed in the violation of the law or nations or a treaty of the United States" (28 U.S.C. 1350). This has evolved into a law that gives foreign nationals an opening to seek justice in U.S. courts for human rights offenses.

However, recent cases interpreting this law by the U.S. Supreme Court have been narrowly interpreted,[184] and show why this law needs to be explicitly expanded to allow foreign nationals and citizens the ability to sue foreign and American corporations for violations of human rights and environmental destruction when the fruits of those crimes (products created by slave labor) end up in the United States.

There are no reasons American consumers cannot have the same options (the right to sue American and foreign corporations) since they have been essentially duped into becoming co-conspirators to these crimes without any redress or ability to fix this injustice. Giving people relief through the legal system to make certain corporations accountable should be at the top of lawmakers' proposals for change in the state and federal arena.

The longer these laws stay the same, the longer this country remains complicit. How we move forward to stop these injustices define us, as a society, for generations to come. We can become the generation that stands up to these problems or allows them to grow. And our lawmakers must assist in ending this once and for all.

In 2016, forward momentum happened when President Barack Obama signed a law that officially banned the import of goods made by forced labor, closing a loophole that had existed for decades, dating back to the 1930s[185] (see Trade Facilitation and Trade Enforcement Act of 2015, ending the loophole provision). The loophole allowed the import of goods made by forced labor if consumer demand could not be met otherwise.

Even though this law closed a loophole that never should have existed, it will mean absolutely nothing if the law is not strictly enforced. Even before this loophole, it was known that common goods such as T-shirts, shoes, and other everyday items made from forced labor and slave labor were imported into the United States. The U.S government itself has reported on this annually in its *List of Goods Produced by Child Labor or Forced Labor*, published by the U.S. Department of Labor Bureau of International Labor Affairs.

*All the laws in the world cannot help stop modern-day slavery and environmental depletion if resources are not devoted to enforce them.*

Even with the loophole closed, it is widely estimated that $142 billion worth of goods made from forced labor are brought into the United States every year. And less than one percent of these are seized or stopped.

A United Nations Working Group on the issue of Human Rights and Transnational Corporations and Other Business found that too many businesses are placing profits over human rights, while governments around the world fail to lead, monitor, and regulate these companies for compliance with basic human rights laws.[186]

According to the report, corporate responsibility regarding human rights should apply to all corporations regardless of size, income, or structure.[187] Businesses are dragging their feet when they could be making the greatest impact to preserve and uphold human rights across the board.[188] "The responsibility to carry out human rights due diligence applies regardless of any 'business case' argument. Failure to conduct adequate diligence on risks to people will often have not only a human cost, but may also come back to haunt the business."[189] Corporate responsibility and due diligence regarding human rights and the environment need to be implemented around the world, with real consequences if they are broken.

In addition to protecting victims of forced labor, we also need to extend greater protection to victims of sex trafficking. The Jeffrey Epstein case brought the issue of sex trafficking to the forefront of almost every media outlet. It was a salacious case of money, greed, and a man who escaped justice for far too long with friends who looked the other way or worse yet helped him exploit minors. The Jeffrey Epstein case showed that sex trafficking can happen in any circle and the assailants can be protected by powerful attorneys and allies (just like corporations).

To create real change, laws need to provide full immunity and protection to victims of sex trafficking so they can come forward to prosecute their accusers. They should be given whistleblower status both legally in criminal and civil courts.

California has been the most proactive in this area. State Senator Scott Wiener sponsored a law that was signed by California Governor Gavin Newsom in 2019.[190] The bill is the first of its kind nationwide, giving victims of sex trafficking the ability to report being a victim or witness of dangerous crimes, including assault, domestic violence, human trafficking, or sexual battery, without fear of arrest or prosecution. This law is a watershed moment in the fight against sex trafficking to help victims build the courage to come forward

Laws to decriminalize the actions of victims tricked or forced into sex work should happen on the state and federal level so all victims can come forward without fear of retaliation or arrest. Until we give victims immunity, this problem will continue to grow and a new generation of young girls will be lured into the dark world of sex trafficking. Girls not even born yet.

It is up to us, the public, to create change across the board for victims of labor and sex trafficking and to demand change for the environment. One of the best ways is by putting pressure on lawmakers to change the laws or enforce the ones on the books in ways that stop these problems instead of helping them grow.

# CHAPTER THIRTEEN

# A GLOBAL CALL TO ACTION

*A small body of determined spirits
fired by an unquenchable faith in their mission
can alter the course of history.*
—*Mahatma Gandhi*

In 2017, the #MeToo movement was named *Time* magazine's Person of the Year. *The Silence Breakers* were honored for their courage and strength in bringing the social problem of sexual assault and harassment in the workplace to a global consciousness. As much as #MeToo has moved the conversation forward, like Black Lives Matter, it is just the beginning.

The #MeToo movement showed the world how women with social status and in many cases extraordinary wealth were not immune to sexual assault or even rape in the workplace. But unlike Hollywood stars, millions of women and children caught in the web of sex trafficking don't have any platform to air their grievances. They don't have Twitter or Instagram accounts followed by millions and routinely patrolled by the worldwide media. They don't have reporters lining up to interview them. They are trapped behind closed doors, scraping together what little they have to buy food for themselves and their families, barely trying to survive.

Maybe it was unexpected that women with high-paying jobs in such public professions were complaining about the very same issues that women who are hidden and silenced have to deal with: equal opportunity, a world free of sexual assault, harassment, and rape.

These two groups couldn't be more different. Yet this tragedy binds them. One group is in the international spotlight, while the other group remains hidden and silenced from the world. Yet both groups desperately want to be heard and create change that is long overdue.

In a profound way, the #MeToo movement showed that sexual assault in the workplace is an issue we all need to care about, regardless of who we are. It impacts people from all spectrums of life. The impact may be disproportionate (with victims of sex trafficking being raped multiple times a day), but the pain is still very real and raw for each survivor.

A letter from the farmworker women of America showed how prevalent this issue is and how united we all can become in changing it:

Dear Sisters,

We write on behalf of the approximately 700,000 women who work in the agricultural fields and packing sheds across the United States. For the past several weeks we have watched and listened with sadness as we have learned of the actors, models and other individuals who have come forward to speak out about the gender based violence they've experienced at the hands of bosses, coworkers and other powerful people in the entertainment industry. We wish that we could say we're shocked to learn that this is such a pervasive problem in your industry. Sadly, we're not surprised because it's a reality we know far too well. Countless farmworker women across our country suffer in silence because of the widespread sexual harassment and assault that they face at work.

We do not work under bright stage lights or on the big screen. We work in the shadows of society in isolated fields and packinghouses that are out of sight and out of mind for most people in this country. Your job feeds souls, fills hearts and spreads joy. Our job nourishes the nation with the fruits, vegetables and other crops that we plant, pick and pack.

Even though we work in very different environments, we share a common experience of being preyed upon by individuals who have the power to hire, fire, blacklist and otherwise threaten our economic, physical and emotional security. Like you, there are few positions available to us and reporting any kind of harm or injustice committed against us doesn't seem like a viable option.

Complaining about anything—even sexual harassment—seems unthinkable because too much is at risk, including the ability to feed our families and preserve our reputations.

We understand the hurt, confusion, isolation and betrayal that you might feel. We also carry shame and fear resulting from this violence. It sits on our backs like oppressive weights. But, deep in our hearts we know that it is not our fault. The only people at fault are the individuals who choose to abuse their power to harass, threaten and harm us, like they have harmed you.

In these moments of despair, and as you cope with scrutiny and criticism because you have bravely chosen to speak out against the harrowing acts that were committed against you, please know that you're not alone. We believe and stand with you.

In solidarity,
Alianza Nacional de Campesinas[191]

The letter eloquently demonstrated why the #MeToo campaign like Black Lives Matter is the beginning to understanding the social injustices that face our world today. These secrets brought to the surface will help stop these abuses.

From profound pain comes hope. And from hope springs the possibility for a better future for people around the world.

Otherwise it's in the atmosphere of secrecy that these social injustices grow. It's one of the primary reasons human trafficking has become a 32 billion dollar a year industry. *If this is not brought out into the open, it will surpass drug trafficking as the world's most lucrative underground industry, if it hasn't already.*

Only when the truth is exposed can the veil of darkness be lifted. Ultimately, we are the ones who can either stop it or turn a blind eye while modern-day social injustices grow. We are either part of the problem or part of the solution. At the end of the day, we decide the answer. We decide how this story turns out with every purchase we make.

## FINAL WORDS: YOU ARE HERE FOR A REASON

Most people live their entire lives never realizing their existence is nothing short of a miracle. Statistically there is a 1 in 400 trillion chance of being born.[192] The fact that you are here is no accident. The fact that you are reading this book is no accident. The fact that your life has brought you to this point is absolutely no accident.

You were born to make an impact, to make a difference in your own way. Let me say this again: *you were born to make an impact*. No matter what the world, family, or friends have told you or how they have made you feel, your life has significant meaning, and you are worthy of a profound life that impacts yourself and others. You deserve to know your worth.

Everything you have been through has brought you to this moment. Every heartache, every lesson, every setback, every defeat has brought you here. People often think they are defined by the events that happened in their past, but that is the furthest from the truth. You are not defined by any event in your past. You are not defined by your family or the culture you were raised in or how you look. The only thing you are defined by is *who you choose to become now and in the future*. You are defined by *who you are*, and those decisions made every day help determine the person you will become and the impact you will leave behind.

You deserve to be part of a movement that changes lives for generations to come. The Red Movement needs you because you are unique and you have special gifts that only you can bring to this world. There is no one exactly like you, and there never will be. And you do make an impact every single day with every single thing you buy. Every buying decision changes lives. And it starts with the daily decisions we often think are so meaningless and mundane. There is absolutely nothing meaningless and mundane about those decisions.

It's been often said that life is not made up of big moments but by small decisions day in and day out that change the trajectory of our lives and the lives of others. Those decisions either reflect who we really are and what we believe, or those decisions are a betrayal to our own sense of self, to our own integrity, to our own understanding of what is right and wrong. It all begins and ends with us.

> You deserve to live a life authentic with your values.

You deserve to know that your presence has made a difference in this world.

You deserve to know that you are enough, flaws and all.

You are more than enough. Our imperfections make us unique.

And this movement needs you, now more than ever.

As a group and individually, we can make profound change and momentum forward, or we can remain silent and complicit in the greatest human rights and environmental crisis in history. What will it be?

As Albert Einstein so powerfully said, "The world will not be destroyed by those who do evil, but by those who watch them without doing anything." Ever wonder what you would have done during the civil rights movement or America's struggle for independence? Who you would have become during those pivotal times in history? You are alive in one of the most crucial times in history now, and what you do and who you become is a matter of choice.

You are deciding your future with every decision you make and every decision you fail to make. These choices create your future and the future of others. We are all agents of change. Every. Single. One. Of. Us.

The sooner we realize that the better.

Every day you are writing your life's story. Every step you take forward is part of your life's book. Make it a story you are proud to be a part of, one filled with courage and hope Ultimately, what good is knowledge without the courage to make a difference in the world? All the knowledge in the world without action is meaningless.

The real revolution is the evolution of our consciousness. Collectively, we can and will change the world. We've seen this happen time and time again in history. Be that agent of change this world so desperately needs, now more than ever.

You are the voice of change. You are the agent for aware-ness. Don't let anyone or anything make you forget that—not the hurts of the past, not the wounds of the present, and defi-nitely not the challenges still ahead.

*If we spend our whole lives focusing on our wounds and what didn't happen for us, we lose out on the opportunity to deliberately create a better future for ourselves and others. We lose out on the gift of life.*

It's not about finding yourself or fixing some old trauma or getting enough therapy so the hurts of the past or your child-hood are undone. It's about going back to the person you were *before the world told you who to be.*

We are the global agents of change. Every. Single. One. Of. Us. And it starts in our own homes, in our own communi-ties, within our own sphere of influence. We are on a journey of monumental change, and the most important question is, "Will you be part of the movement forward, or will you stay stuck?" Only you can answer that question.

The world needs you, now more than ever.

You are part of the global call to action, every single one of you reading this today.

Start now. Start today.
The world is waiting.
We have just begun…

# ENDNOTES

CHAPTER ONE: THE HIDDEN SIDE OF CHOCOLATE

1. Tiger, Caroline. "Bittersweet Chocolate." *Salon*. Published February 14, 2003. Available at: http://www.laborrights.org/in-the-news/bittersweet-chocolate

2. *The Dark Side of Chocolate*. Directed by Miki Mistrati 2010; Denmark: Bastard Film & TV, 2010. Film. Available at: https://topdocumentaryfilms.com/dark-side-chocolate/

3. Id.

4. Id.

5. Id.

6. Ryan, Orla. "Chocolate Nations: Living and Dying for Cocoa in West Africa." London, UK and New York, NY, USA: Zed Books, 2011.

7. Id.

8. Jeffery, Simon and Stafford, Ben. "Slavery: the chocolate companies have their say." *The Guardian*. Published April 19, 2001. Available at: https://www.theguardian.com/world/2001/apr/19/globalisation.benstafford. Last Accessed March 18, 2018; Fearon, Peter, "Cocoa Farmers Harbor a Dark Secret: Slavery." *The New York Post*. Published May 10, 2001. Available at: https://nypost.com/2001/05/10/cocoa-farmers-harbor-a-dark-secret-slavery/

9. Parenti, Christian. "Chocolate's bittersweet economy." *Nigerian Muse*. Published February 15, 2008. Available at: http://www.nigerianmuse.com/20080217065523zg/nigeria-watch/chocolates-bittersweet-economy-by-christian-parenti-fortune-magazine/

10. Id.

11. Id.

12. Id.

13. Id.

14. "Cocoa Barometer 2018 Report." Fountain, A.C. and Hütz-Adams, F. (2018) https://www.voicenetwork.eu/wp-content/uploads/2019/08/Cocoaborometer2018_web4.pdf

15. "Third Annual Report: Oversight of Public and Private Initiatives to Eliminate the Worst Forms of Child Labor in the Cocoa Sector in Cote d'Ivoire and Ghana." *Payson Center for International Development and Technology Transfer Tulane University*. Published September 30, 2009. Available at: http://www.childlaborcocoa.org/images/Payson_Reports/Third_Annual_Report.pdf

16. Id.

17. Ryan. *Chocolate Nations, supra* note 6.

18. "About the International Cocoa Initiative." *International Cocoa Initiative Foundation*. Available at: http://www.cocoainitiative.org/about-ici/about-us/

19. Id.

20. *Doe v. Nestle*, 748 F.Supp.2d 1057 (2010) United States District Court, C.D. California. September 8, 2010. Available at https://scholar.google.com/scholar_case?case=13856676954338814599&q=doe+v.+nestle&hl=en&as_sdt=4,321,322,323,324

21. "Nestlé, Cargill, Archer Daniels Midland lawsuit (re Côte d'Ivoire)." *Business & Human Rights Resource Centre*. Available at: https://business-humanrights.org/en/nestl%C3%A9-cargill-archer-daniels-midland-lawsuit-re-c%C3%B4te-divoire

22. Id.

23. *John DOE I; John Doe II; John Doe III, individually and on behalf of proposed class members; Global Exchange*, Plaintiffs–Appellants, v. *NESTLE USA, INC.; Archer Daniels Midland Company; Cargill Incorporated Company; Cargill Cocoa*, Defendants–Appellees (September 4, 2014). Available at: http://caselaw.findlaw.com/us-9th-circuit/1677180.html

24. Id.

25. Id.

26. Id.

27. Id.

28. Id,

29. *Business & Human Rights Resource Centre, supra* note 21.

30. Id.

31. Basso, Karina. "Hershey, Nestle, and Mars Sued in Child Slavery Class Action." *Top Class Actions, LLC*. Published Sept. 30, 2015. Available at: https://topclassactions.com/lawsuit-settlements/lawsuit-news/176537-hershey-nestle-and-mars-sued-in-child-slavery-class-action/

32. *Hodson v. Mars Inc.*, Case No. 3:15-cv-04450 (N.D. Cal.). Available at: https://www.consumerproductmatters.com/wp-content/uploads/sites/13/2016/03/Hodsdon-v.-Mars.pdf

33. Basso, Karina. "Hershey, Nestle, and Mars Sued in Child Slavery Class Action." *Top Class Actions, LLC*. Published Sept. 30, 2015. Available at: https://topclassactions.com/lawsuit-settlements/lawsuit-news/176537-hershey-nestle-and-mars-sued-in-child-slavery-class-action/

34. Id.

35.  Cote d'Ivoire: Fair Labor Association report finds child labour in Nestlé's cocoa supply chain;" *Business & Human Rights Resource Centre*. Available at: https://www.business-humanrights.org/en/cote-divoire-fair-labor-association-report-finds-child-labour-in-nestlés-cocoa-supply-chain-includes-company-comments

36.  Id.

37.  Id.

38.  Id.

39.  Davis, Christina. "Nestle, Hershey Class Action Child Slavery Lawsuit Dismissed." *Top Class Actions, LLC*. Published March 31, 2016. Available at: https://topclassactions.com/lawsuit-settlements/lawsuit-news/331645-nestle-hershey-class-action-child-slavery-lawsuit-dismissed/

CHAPTER TWO: WHAT IS THE RED MOVEMENT?

40.  At a news conference in Vatican City on November 14, 2006, Cardinal Renato Martino, a former Vatican envoy to the United Nations and head of the Holy See Office, revealed that modern-day slavery is "worse than the slavery of those taken from Africa and brought to other countries." The cardinal also said, "In a world which proclaims human rights left and right, let's see what it does about the rights of so many human beings which are not respected but trampled." The cardinal released an annual papal message concerning problems faced by these victims and the need to protect them.

41.  Id.

42.  Scholars estimate that during the transatlantic slave trade more than 12 million Africans were sold into slavery. The number of people living in slave-like conditions today is over 40 million worldwide.

43.  It has been widely reported in the media and academic articles that human trafficking is a $32 billion-a-year industry that is more profitable than Starbucks, Amazon, and Google combined.

44. List of Goods Produced by Child Labor or Forced Labor." *United State Department of Labor, Bureau of International Labor Affairs.*

CHAPTER THREE: IT IS EVERYWHERE

45. For more information see "Oversight of Public and Private Initiatives to Eliminate the Worst Forms of Child Labor in the Cocoa Sector in Cote d'Ivoire and Ghana." *Payson Center for International Development and Technology Transfer Tulane University.* Published March 31, 2011. Available at: https://www.dol.gov/ilab/issues/child-labor/cocoa/Tulane_Final_Report.pdf

or https://issuu.com/stevebutton/docs/tulane_final_report

"Coffee Drinking Statistics." *Statistic Brain Research Institute.* Published 2016. Available at: http://www.statisticbrain.com/coffee-drinking-statistics/

46. Gresser, Charis and Tickell, Sophia. "Mugged: Poverty in Your Cup." *Oxfam America.* Published December 10, 2004. Available at: https://www.oxfamamerica.org/explore/research-publications/mugged-poverty-in-your-coffee-cup/

47. Id.

48. Id.

49. "International Child Labor & Forced Labor Reports." *United States Department of Labor, Bureau of International Labor Affairs.* Available at: https://www.dol.gov/agencies/ilab/reports/child-labor

("ILAB publishes three reports on international child labor and forced labor that serve as valuable resources for research, advocacy, government action and corporate responsibility. These reports are: The Department of Labor's Findings on the Worst Forms of Child Labor; the List of Goods Produced by Child Labor or Forced Labor; and the List of Products Produced by Forced or Indentured Child Labor. Each of these reports has a distinct mandate, focus and set of implications, but taken collectively, they document the current situation of child labor, forced labor and forced child labor around the world."); "U.S. Labor Department Issues Report On Labor

Concerns In Dominican Sugar Sector, Announces $10 Million Project In Agriculture." United States Department of Labor, Bureau of International Labor Affairs. Available at: https://www.dol.gov/newsroom/releases/ilab/ilab20131979. ("The Bureau of International Labor Affairs leads the U.S. Department of Labor's efforts to ensure that workers around the world are treated fairly and are able to share in the benefits of the global economy.")

50. "2015 Findings on the Worst Forms of Child Labor." *United States Department of Labor, Bureau of International Labor Affairs.* Published 2015. Available at: https://www.dol.gov/sites/default/files/documents/ilab/reports/child-labor/findings/2015TDA_1.pdf

The U.S. Department of Labor's report tracks the worst forms of child labor around the world.

51. "List of Goods Produced by Child Labor or Forced Labor." *United State Department of Labor, Bureau of International Labor Affairs.* Published September 2016. Available at: https://www.dol.gov/ilab/reports/child-labor/list-of-goods/

52. "List of Goods Produced by Child Labor or Forced Labor." *United State Department of Labor, Bureau of International Labor Affairs.* Published September 2018. Available at: https://www.dol.gov/agencies/ilab/reports/child-labor/list-of-goods

53. Id.

54. Id.

CHAPTER FOUR: BLOOD DIAMONDS

55. "About." *Kimberley Process.* Available at: https://www.kimberleyprocess.com/en/about.

56. Id.

57. "Conflict diamonds, also known as 'blood' diamonds, are rough diamonds used by rebel movements or their allies to finance armed conflicts aimed at undermining legitimate governments."

"What is the KP/FAQ." Kimberley Process. Available at: https://www. kimberleyprocess.com/en/faq

58. Id.

59. "Our Ethical Practices." *Brilliant Earth.* Published 2017. Available at: http://www.brilliantearth.com/why-buy-from-brilliant-earth/

60. China Labor Watch (also known as CLW) is a non-profit company that strives to expose the transparency of labor conditions in factories along with the reality of their supply chains while advocating for worker's rights and supporting the labor movement in China. More information can be found at www.chinalaborwatch.org

61. China Labor Watch, "The Other Side of Fairy Tale: An Investigation of Labor Conditions at Five Chinese Toy Factories." Published November 20, 2015. Available at http://www.chinalaborwatch.org/upfile/2015_11_20/2015.11.20%20The%20Other%20Side%20of%20Fairy%20Tales%20-%20EN%20final.small.pdf

62. Id.

63. Id.

64. Id.

65. Id. at p. 2 of Executive Summary.

66. Id.

67. China Labor Watch, "The Dark Side of the Toy World, Published November 27, 2017. Available at http://www.chinalaborwatch.org/upfile/2017_11_27/Toy%20Investigation%20Report%201127.pdf

CHAPTER FIVE: FAST FASHION, MODERN-DAY SLAVERY, AND THE ENVIRONMENTAL FALLOUT

68. Walk Free Foundation, *The Global Slavery Index 2018*. Western Australia: Walk Free Foundation Publication 2018 through the Minderoo Foundation Pty Ltd. Available at: https://downloads.globalslaveryindex.org/ephemeral/GSI-2018_FNL_180907_Digital-small-p-1542636484.pdf.

https://i-d.vice.com/en_us/article/a3qk7e/a-new-report-says-the-fashion-industry-is-fueling-modern-slavery

https://www.minderoo.org/walk-free/?utm_medium=301&utm_source=www.minderoo.com.au

69. *Walk Free Foundation*. supra 68.

70. California Transparency in Supply Chains Act of 2010, Senate Bill No. 657, Chapter 556, Available at https://oag.ca.gov/sites/all/files/agweb/pdfs/cybersafety/sb_657_bill_ch556.pdf.

71. *Walk Free Foundation*, supra 68.

72. ABLE Fashion Brand website. Available at https://www.livefashionable.com/pages/about-able

73. ABLE Fashion Brand website. Our Wages. Available at https://www.livefashionable.com/pages/our-wages

CHAPTER SIX: ELECTRONICS

74. In May 2012, a Hong Kong based non-profit called Students and Scholars Against Corporate Misbehavior (SACOM) published a report that illustrated labor violations and dangerous conditions in Foxconn factories in the Chinese cities of Shenzhen and Zhengzhou. This report was widely circulated partly because of its connection to Apple products. As a supplier of Apple, this report revealed some of the inherent problems in the supply chain of common electronics used by consumers around the world. Since the report, SACOM has published other investigative reports

regarding labor and working conditions in the electronics, fashion and the toy industries. See http://sacom.hk/category/information-centre/investigative-report/

75. The May 2012 report by SACOM referenced above interviewed over 170 Foxconn workers and detailed how 20 to 30 people had been housed in three-bedroom apartments.

76. Dr. J. Mayford is not his real name. For purposes of privacy, his name has been changed.

77. Apple Supplier Responsibility website. Available at https://www.apple.com/supplier-responsibility/

78. Id.

79. Id.

80. Apple 2019 Progress Report. Available at https://www.apple.com/supplier-responsibility/pdf/Apple_SR_2019_Progress_Report.pdf

81. Id.

82. Id at p. 55.

83. Verité. *Forced Labor in the Production of Electronic Goods in Malaysia.* Verite Publication September 2014. Available a: https://verite.org/wp-content/uploads/2016/11/VeriteForcedLaborMalaysianElectronics2014.pdf.

In 2012, Verité received funding from the U.S. Department of Labor to conduct an investigation to evaluate whether forced labor existed in the electronics industry in Malaysia and at what prevalence. This study had far reaching consequences and analyses at how electronics can be traced around the world because of the varied component parts in the devices that have various supply chains. In some cases, it's difficult to pinpoint where one supply chain starts and another ends. Due to the varied nature, it increases the risk of electronics being tainted by some form of modern-day slavery in its production.

84. Id at page 27.

85. Id.

86. Id page 26.

87. Id page 29–30.

88. Id.

89. Id at page 86–87.

90. Id at page 87.

91. Amnesty International. *Trapped: The Exploitation of Migrant Workers in Malaysia. London.* Amnesty International. March 2010. https://www.amnesty.org/download/Documents/36000/asa280022010en.pdf.

Centre for Research on Multinational Corporations (SOMO): Outsourcing labour: Migrant labour rights in Malaysia's electronics industry (Amsterdam, Jan. 2013).

S. Bormann, P. Krishnan and M. F. Neuner: Migration in a digital age— Migrant workers in the Malaysian electronics industry: A case study on Jabil Circuit and Flextronics (Berlin, WEED, December 2010).

National Human Rights Commission, Nepal (NHRC): Human rights situation of Nepalese migrant workers: Observation and monitoring report, South Korea and Malaysia (Kathmandu, Dec. 2013). Also available at http://www.nhrcnepal.org/nhrc_new/doc/newsletter/HR%20 situation%20 of%20Nepalese%20Migrant%20Worker%20Report%20 Aug30-Sept7-2013.pdf.

92. Verite. *Forced Labor in the Production of Electronic Goods in Malaysia.* Verite Publication September 2014, page 108. Available at https://verite.org/wp-content/uploads/2016/11/VeriteForcedLaborMalaysianElectronics2014.pdf

93. Id at page 128.

94. Ibid.

95. Ibid.

96. Amnesty International. *Trapped: The Exploitation of Migrant Workers in Malaysia. London.* Amnesty International. March 2010. https://www.amnesty.org/download/Documents/36000/asa280022010en.pdf

97. S. Bormann, P. Krishnan and M.E. Neuner: Migration in a digital age—Migrant workers in the Malaysian electronics industry: A case study on Jabil Circuit and Flextronics (Berlin, WEED, December 2010).

98. Centre for Research on Multinational Corporations (SOMO): Outsourcing labour: Migrant labour rights in Malaysia's electronics industry (Amsterdam, Jan. 2013).

99. Verite. *Forced Labor in the Production of Electronic Goods in Malaysia.* Verite Publication September 2014. Available a: https://verite.org/wp-content/uploads/2016/11/VeriteForcedLaborMalaysianElectronics2014.pdf.

100. Id.

101. *Verite*, supra note 92, page 3 Acknowledgment Section.

CHAPTER SEVEN: HOW DID WE GET HERE?

102. "List of Goods Produced by Child Labor or Forced Labor." *United State Department of Labor, Bureau of International Labor Affairs.* Published September 2018. Available at:https://www.dol.gov/agencies/ilab/reports/child-labor/list-of-goods

103. Id.

104. Gus Lubin, There's a Staggering Conspiracy Behind the Rise of Consumer Culture," *Business Insider*, February 23, 2013. Available at https://www.businessinsider.com/birth-of-consumer-culture-2013-2

105. Id.

106. Id.

107. Id.

108. Id.

109. Michelle Alexander, *The New Jim Crow* (New York: The New Press, Tenth Anniversary Edition);

See Results from the 2002 National Survey on Drug Use and Health; National Findings. NHSDA series H-22. DHHS pub. no. SMA03-3836 showed the illegal drug use amount white and blacks to be very similar. These findings were also concluded in the U.S. Department of Health and Human Services, Substance Abuse and Mental Health Services, Summary of Findings from the 2000 National Household Survey on Drug Abuse and again confirmed in the Results from the 2007 National Survey on Drug Use and Health: National Findings. DHHS publications.

110. U.S. Has World's Highest Incarceration Rate – Population Reference Bureau (prb.org). Available at www.prb.org/us-incarceration/

See also Becky Pettit, *Invisible Men: Mass Incarceration and the Myth of Black Progress* (New York: Russell Sage Foundation: 2012)

111. U.S. Rates of Incarceration: A Global Perspective from National Council on Crime and Delinquency. Fact Sheet by Christopher Hartney Available at www.evidentchange.org/sites/default/files/publication_pdf/factsheet-us-incarceration.pdf

112. Neiman Watchdog, "Does Mass Incarceration Make Us Safer?" Available at www.niemanwatchdog.org/index.cfm?fuseaction=ask_this.view&askthisid=301

(Harvard sociologist Bruce Western's research revealed that the historical attempt to increase public safety through an increasing dependence on imprisonment and mass incarceration likely had the opposite effect by undermining inner city families, leaving black communities destitute, and keeping those communities and a generation of black men from having access to opportunities and resources available to other groups.)

113. Robert E. Lane, *Political Ideology: Why the American Common Man Believes What He Does* (New York: The Free Press, 1962), p. 80.

114. Stewart Ewen, Captains of Consciousness: Advertising and the Social Roots of the Consumer Culture (New York; McGraw-Hill, 1976), pp. 70, 108.

115. A 2019 report called "Plastic & Climate the Hidden Costs of a Plastic Planet," by the Center for International Environmental Law (CIEL) states that the increase of plastic in our environment threatens climate change. "At current levels, greenhouse gas emissions from the plastic lifecycle threaten the ability of the global community to keep global temperature rise below 1.5 degree Celsius. With the petrochemical and plastic industries planning a massive expansion in production, the problem is on track to get much worse." Executive summary available at https://www.ciel.org/wp-content/uploads/2019/05/Plastic-and-Climate-Executive-Summary-2019.pdf. Full report available at https://www.ciel.org/plasticandclimate/

116. CHAPTER EIGHT: THE SECRET BEHIND THE SUPER BOWL

FBI New York Field Office. *Sixteen Juveniles Recovered In Joint Super Bowl Operation Targeting Underage Prostitution.;* 2014. Available at: https://www.fbi.gov/newyork/press-releases/2014/sixteen-juveniles-recovered-in-joint-super-bowl-operation-targeting-underage-prostitution

117. Id.

118. Id.

119. The Voice of Black Cincinnati, Statistics are quoted from their informational website. Available at thevoiceofblackcincinnati.com/african-american-human-trafficking/

120. United Nations, *Protocol to Prevent, Suppress, and Punish Trafficking in Persons, Especially Women and Children, Supplementing the United Nations*

*Convention against Transnational Organized Crime* (New York: United Nations, 2000).

121. Latonero, Mark, *Human Trafficking Online: The Role of Social Networking Sites and Online Classifieds.* Available at SSRN: http://ssrn.com/abstract=2045851

122. Id.

123. STOPP Website Staff, "Online Gaming: The Newest Weapon of Human Traffickers," December 7, 2018 http://stopptrafficking.com/online-gaming-the-newest-weapon-of-human-traffickers-part-1/

http://sharedhope.org/wp-content/uploads/2019/10/Video-Games-and-Gaming-Factsheet.pdf

For further information, visit the *Tampa Bay Times* article "Human Traffickers' New Tool to Lure Children: Online Video Games," available at https://www.tampabay.com/news/publicsafety/human-traffickers-new-tool-to-lure-children-online-video-games-20190121/

124. For her privacy, the survivor's name and certain details have been changed. Interviews with the survivor of human trafficking were conducted in Chicago, Illinois, in 2012–13 by Shadan Kapri.

125. Andrea J. Sedlak, David Finkelhor, Heather Hammer, and Dana J. Schultz, *National Estimates of Missing Children: An Overview* (Washington, D.C: U.S. Department of Justice, Office of Justice Programs, 2002), https://www.ncjrs.gov/pdffiles1/ojjdp/196465.pdf

126. Interview with Rachel Ramirez, an organizer with the Chicago Coalition for the Homeless, Chicago, Illinois, November 1, 2012. Interview conducted by Shadan Kapri.

127. National Human Trafficking Resource Center. The Victims. 2014. Available at: https://traffickingresourcecenter.org/what-human-trafficking/human-trafficking/victims

CHAPTER NINE: THE WORLD CUP AND MODERN-DAY SLAVERY

128.  Amnesty International. *The Dark Side of Migration: Spotlight on Qatar's Construction Sector ahead of the World Cup* (London: Amnesty International Publications, 2013), http://www.amnestyusa.org/sites/default/files/mde220102013eng.pdf;

Human Rights Watch, "*World Report 2012: Qatar.* New York, NY: Human Rights Watch Available at: https://www.hrw.org/world-report/2012/country-chapters/qatar

129.  Lillie, Michele. "Sex Trafficking at the FIFA World Cup in Brazil," *Human Trafficking Search: The Global Resource and Database,* Published July 14, 2014. Available at: http://humantraffickingsearch.net/wp/sex-trafficking-at-the-fifa-world-cup-in-brazil/

130.  *See* Goldberg, Eleanor Goldberg. "Children Sold for Sex at World Cup for Few Dollars, Pack of Cigarettes." *Huffington Post Impact*, Published June 12, 2014. Available at: https://www.huffpost.com/entry/world-cup-child-prostitution_n_5474716?guccounter=1

131.  Lillie, Michele. "Sex Trafficking at the FIFA World Cup in Brazil," *Human Trafficking Search: The Global Resource and Database,* Published July 14, 2014. Available at: http://humantraffickingsearch.net/wp/sex-trafficking-at-the-fifa-world-cup-in-brazil/

132.  Id.

133.  Id.

134.  Sister Gabriella Bottani, Italian nun who helped organize a coalition against trafficking involving 79 countries and 240 religious congregations quoted in *CBS News Online.* Quote from a press conference at the Vatican. Available at: http://www.cbsnews.com/news/nuns-to-combat-child-prostitution-at-world-cup-2014/

135.  Patel, Keshar. "Sex Trafficking Sullies World Cup," *World Policy Blog*, Available at: http://www.worldpolicy.org/blog/2014/06/17/sex-trafficking-sullies-world-cup.

136.  "Sixteen Additional FIFA Officials Indicted for Racketeering Conspiracy and Corruption." *Justice.Gov*, 2017. https://www.justice.gov/opa/pr/sixteen-additional-fifa-officials-indicted-racketeering-conspiracy-and-corruption

137.  Amnesty International. *The Dark Side of Migration: Spotlight on Qatar's Construction Sector Ahead of the World Cup.* London: Amnesty International Publications 2013; 2013. Available at: http://www.amnestyusa.org/sites/default/files/mde220102013eng.pdf

138.  Amnesty International. *The Dark Side of Migration: Spotlight on Qatar's Construction Sector Ahead of The World Cup.* London: Amnesty International Publications 2013; 2013. Available at: http://www.amnestyusa.org/sites/default/files/mde220102013eng.pdf. Last Accessed September 23, 2019; Human Rights Watch. *World Report 2012: Qatar.* New York, NY: Human Rights Watch Available at: https://www.hrw.org/world-report/2012/country-chapters/qatar

139.  Id.

140.  Id.

141.  Id.

142.  Ibid, Human Rights Watch. *World Report 2012: Qatar.* New York, NY: Human Rights Watch Available at: https://www.hrw.org/world-report/2012/country-chapters/qatar

143.  Amnesty International. *The Dark Side of Migration: Spotlight on Qatar's Construction Sector Ahead of The World Cup.* London: Amnesty International Publications 2013; 2013. Available at: http://www.amnestyusa.org/sites/default/files/mde220102013eng.pdf

144. Sharan Burrow quoted in Greg Wilesmith and Eric Campbell's, "Qatar 2022: World Cup project workers living in slum conditions behind glitz of oil-rich country," *ABC News Online*, Updated July 14, 2015. Available at: http://www.abc.net.au/news/2015-06-02/investigation-into-qatar-2022-reveals-exploitation-of-workers/6511660

145. *See* Human Rights Watch, *World Report 2012*; International, *The Dark Side of Migration: Spotlight on Qatar's Construction Sector Ahead of The World Cup.*

146. Lobel, Mark. "Arrested for Reporting on Qatar's World Cup Labourers." *BBC News*, Published May 18 2015. Available at: http://www.bbc.com/news/world-middle-east-32775563. Last Accessed October 1, 2019; Greg Wilesmith and Eric Campbell, "Qatar's World Cup of censorship on display," *ABC News Online*, Published June 1, 2015. Available at: http://www.abc.net.au/news/2015-06-02/wilesmith-campell-qatar's-world-cup-of-censorship-on-display/6515012

147. Lobel, Mark. "Arrested for Reporting on Qatar's World Cup Labourers." *BBC News*, Published May 18 2015. Available at: http://www.bbc.com/news/world-middle-east-32775563

148. Video: Foreign Correspondent takes a look inside the living quarters of Qatar 2022 workers. *ABC News*, Updated July 14, 2015. Foreign Correspondents Greg Wilesmith and Eric Campbell. Available at: http://www.abc.net.au/news/2015-06-02/investigation-into-qatar-2022-reveals-exploitation-of-workers/6511660

149. Id.

150. Qatar's Government Communication Office. *Qatar's Government Communication Office Denies Washington Post Article About Worker Conditions in Qatar.*; Published June 2, 2015. Available at: http://www.usqbc.org/news/qatars-government-communications-office-denies-washington-post-article-about-worker-conditions-in-qatar

151. Ingraham, Christopher. "(UPDATED) The toll of human causalities in Qatar," *Washington Post Online*, Updated May 27, 2015. Available at: https://

www.washingtonpost.com/news/wonk/wp/2015/05/27/a-body-count-in-qatar-illustrates-the-consequences-of-fifa-corruption/

CHAPTER TEN: THE OLYMPICS AND HUMAN TRAFFICKING

152. "Olympic Games Candidature Process." *International Olympic Committee.* Available at: http://www.olympic.org/all-about-the-candidature-process

153. Mallon, Bill, M.D. "The Olympic Bribery Scandal." *Journal of Olympic History.* International Society of Olympic Historians. Published May 2000: 11-27. Available at: http://library.la84.org/SportsLibrary/JOH/JOHv8n2/johv8n2f.pdf

154. Id.

155. Id.

156. Human Rights Watch. "Race to the Bottom: Exploitation of Migrant Workers Ahead of Russia's 2014 Winter Olympic Games in Sochi." *Human Rights Watch.* Published 2013: 17. Available at: https://www.hrw.org/sites/default/files/reports/russia0213_ForUpload.pdf "The President of the Sochi 2014 Organizing Committee has called the 2014 Olympics preparations 'the largest [construction] project in Russia's history.'"

157. Id.

158. Id.

159. Id.

160. Id.

161. Id.

162. Id.

163. Kangaspunta, Kristina. "Mapping the inhuman trade: Preliminary findings of the database on trafficking in human beings." *UNODC Forum on Crime and Society*, 3 (1 & 2) 2003: 82-83. Available at:

http://www.unodc.org/pdf/crime/forum/forum3.pdf#page=85

164. Shaw, Craig, Roman Anin, and Lina Vdovii. "Ghosts of Sochi: Hundreds Killed in Olympic Construction." *The Black Sea*. Last modified January 6, 2015. Available at:

https://theblacksea.eu/stories/ghosts-of-sochi/

165. Id.

166. Id.

167. Id.

168. Ibid. (Mahsud Abdujabbarov was the head of the Interregional Center for Education of Migrants in Moscow. After he published reports of migrant deaths in Russia, he spent two months in jail, was kicked out of Russia and fled Uzbekistan and is in hiding.).

169. Id.

170. "Trafficking in Persons Report." *U.S. Department of State*. Published June 2013: 310. Available at: https://www.state.gov/documents/organization/210741.pdf

171. Human Rights Watch. "Race to the Bottom: Exploitation of Migrant Workers Ahead of Russia's 2014 Winter Olympic Games in Sochi." *Human Rights Watch*. Published 2013. Available at: https://www.hrw.org/sites/default/files/reports/russia0213_ForUpload.pdf

172. Id.

173. Id.

174. Human Rights Watch. "One Year of My Blood: Exploitation of Migrant Construction Workers in Beijing." *Human Rights Watch*. Published March 2008. Available at: https://www.hrw.org/sites/default/files/reports/china0308webwcover.pdf

175. "Olympic Charter." *International Olympic Committee.* Available at: https://stillmed.olympic.org/media/Document%20Library/OlympicOrg/Olympic-Studies-Centre/List-of-Resources/Official-Publications/Olympic-Charters/EN-2013-Olympic-Charter.pdf#_ga=2.14815797.2011197199.1495221762-1879524367.1495221123

176. Kielburger, Craig and Marc Kielburger. "Human Rights in Sochi: If Exploited Migrant Workers Built It, Should the World Still Come?" *Huffington Post.* Last modified April 12, 2014. Available at: http://www.huffingtonpost.ca/craig-and-marc-kielburger/human-rights-in-sochi_b_4747464.html

177. "Russia: IOC Acts on Sochi Abuses," *Human Rights Watch.* Available at https://www.hrw.org/news/2014/02/11/russia-ioc-acts-sochi-abuses#

178. Id.

179. See Olympic Charter. *International Olympic Committee.* Available at: https://stillmed.olympic.org/media/Document%20Library/OlympicOrg/Olympic-Studies-Centre/List-of-Resources/Official-Publications/Olympic-Charters/EN-2013-Olympic-Charter.pdf#_ga=2.14815797.2011197199.1495221762-1879524367.1495221123

CHAPTER ELEVEN: SOLUTIONS TO A GLOBAL EPIDEMIC

180. The Branded Collective story. Available at www.brandedcollective.com/pages/story

CHAPTER TWELVE: NEW LEGAL AND SOCIAL FRAMEWORKS

181. U.S. Constitution Thirteenth Amendment ("Neither slavery nor involuntary servitude, except as a punishment for crime whereof the party shall have been duly convicted, shall exist within the United States, or any place subject to their jurisdiction.")

182. The California Transparency in Supply Chains Act of 2010 went into effect on January 1, 2012 only in the State of California. This state law is also known as SB657. This law is a good start since it requires disclosure

of corporations' efforts or policies in eliminating human trafficking from their supply chain. The law does not require any corporations to adopt any specific policy related to human trafficking and slavery in their supply chain. This is where the law falls short in that it doesn't require real action but just disclosure of action, if any is present.

The next generation of laws aimed at fighting human trafficking should require corporations to reveal what actions they are taking and the impact they are having in addition to adopting specific known policies and procedures that will decrease the prevalence of slavery in their supply chain. This should apply for all manufacturers and retailers doing business (large or small). Currently, this Act only applies to 1) retailers or companies; 2) doing business in the State of California who have; 3) annual gross revenue over 100 million dollars. The high amount of gross profits needed to require such reporting is another weakness of the law and should be amended to include any company doing business in California or selling their products there.

183. The most recent version of the proposed Business Supply Chain Transparency Act 2018. Available at https://www.congress.gov/bill/115th-congress/house-bill/7089/text.

See text of bill below.

A bill to amend the Securities Exchange Act of 1934 to require certain companies to disclose information describing any measures the company has taken to identify and address conditions of forced labor, slavery, human trafficking, and the worst forms of child labor within the company's supply chains.

*Be it enacted by the Senate and House of Representatives of the United States of America in Congress assembled,*

## SECTION 1. Short title.

This Act may be cited as the "Business Supply Chain Transparency on Trafficking and Slavery Act of 2018."

## SEC. 2. Findings and sense of Congress.

(a) Findings.——Congress finds the following:

(1) In 2014, the Department of Labor identified 136 goods from 74 countries around the world made by forced labor and child labor.

(2) The United States is the world's largest importer, and in the 21st century, investors, consumers, and broader civil society increasingly demand information about the human rights impact of products in the United States market.

(3) Courts have ruled that consumers do not have standing to bring a civil action in United States courts for enforcement of a provision in the Smoot Hawley Tariff Act of 1930 prohibiting importation of goods made with forced labor or convict labor, and furthermore, the provision has a broad exception for goods that cannot be produced in the United States in sufficient quantities to meet the demands of American consumers from tainted goods, consequently, there are fewer than 40 enforcement actions on record in the past 80 years.

(4) Mechanisms under Federal law to prevent and punish perpetrators of forced labor, slavery, human trafficking, and the worst forms of child labor in the stream of commerce suffer from problems of limited scope, broad expectations, and lack of available information about goods that are produced along supply chains tainted by these crimes and imported by the United States.

(5) The Trafficking Victims Protection Reauthorization Act of 2003 (Public Law 108–193) together with the Trafficking Victims Protection Act of 2005 (Public Law 109–164) provide for the termination of Federal contracts where a Federal contractor or subcontractor engages in severe forms of trafficking in persons or has procured a commercial sex act during the period of time that the grant, contract, or cooperative agreement is in effect, or uses forced labor in the performance of the grant, contract, or

cooperative agreement. The Trafficking Victims Protection Act of 2005 also provides United States courts with criminal jurisdiction abroad over Federal employees, contractors, or subcontractors who participate in severe forms of trafficking in persons or forced labor.

(6) Executive Order 13126, Prohibition of Acquisition of Products Produced by Forced or Indentured Child Labor, Executive Order 13627, Strengthening Protections Against Trafficking In Persons In Federal Contracts, and title XVII of the National Defense Authorization Act for Fiscal Year 2013 (Public Law 112–239) have prohibited Federal contractors, subcontractors, and their employees from engaging in the following trafficking-related activities: charging labor recruitment fees; confiscating passports and other identity documents of workers; and using fraudulent recruitment practices, including failing to disclose basic information or making material misrepresentations about the terms and conditions of employment. Such Executive order and Acts also require Federal contractors, subcontractors, and their employees to maintain an anti-trafficking compliance plan that includes, among other elements, a complaint mechanism and procedures to prevent subcontractors at any tier in the supply chain from engaging in trafficking in persons.

(b) Sense of Congress.—It is the sense of Congress that—

(1) forced labor, slavery, human trafficking, and the worst forms of child labor are among the most egregious forms of abuse that humans commit against each other, for the sake of commercial profit;

(2) the legislative and regulatory framework to prevent goods produced by forced labor, slavery, human trafficking, and the worst forms of child labor from passing into the stream of commerce in the United States is gravely inadequate;

(3) legislation is necessary to provide consumers information on products that are free of child labor, forced labor, slavery, and human trafficking; and

(4) through publicly available disclosures, businesses and consumers can avoid inadvertently promoting or sanctioning these crimes through production and purchase of raw materials, goods and finished products that have been tainted in the supply chains.

## SEC. 3. Disclosure of information relating to efforts to combat the Use of Forced Labor, Slavery, Trafficking in Persons, or the Worst Forms of Child Labor.

Section 13 of the Securities Exchange Act of 1934 (15 U.S.C. 78m) is amended by adding at the end the following new subsection:

"(s) Disclosures relating to efforts To combat the Use of Forced Labor, Slavery, Trafficking in Persons, or the Worst Forms of Child Labor.—

"(1) REGULATIONS.—Not later than 1 year after the date of enactment of the Business Supply Chain Transparency on Trafficking and Slavery Act of 2018, the Commission, in consultation with the Secretary of State, shall promulgate regulations to require that any covered issuer required to file reports with the Commission under this section to include annually in such reports, a disclosure whether the covered issuer has taken any measures during the year for which such reporting is required to identify and address conditions of forced labor, slavery, human trafficking, and the worst forms of child labor within the covered issuer's supply chain, and a description of such measures taken. Such disclosure shall include, under the heading 'Policies to Address Forced Labor, Slavery, Human Trafficking, and the Worst Forms of Child Labor', information describing to what extent, if any, the covered issuer conducts any of the following activities:

*Endnotes*

"(A) Whether the covered issuer maintains a policy to identify and eliminate the risks of forced labor, slavery, human trafficking, and the worst forms of child labor within the covered issuer's supply chain (such disclosure to include the text of the policy or substantive description of the elements of the policy), and actions the covered issuer has taken pursuant to or in the absence of such policy.

"(B) Whether the covered issuer maintains a policy prohibiting its employees and employees of entities associated with its supply chain from engaging in commercial sex acts with a minor.

"(C) The efforts of the covered issuer to evaluate and address the risks of forced labor, slavery, human trafficking, and the worst forms of child labor in the product supply chain. If such efforts have been made, such disclosure shall—

>"(i) describe any risks identified within the supply chain, and the measures taken toward eliminating those risks;
>
>"(ii) specify whether the evaluation was or was not conducted by a third party;
>
>"(iii) specify whether the process includes consultation with the independent labor organizations (as such term is defined in section 2 of the National Labor Relations Act (29 U.S.C. 152)), workers' associations, or workers within workplaces and incorporates the resulting input or written comments from such independent labor organizations, workers' associations, or workers and if so, the disclosure shall describe

the entities consulted and specify the method of such consultation; and

"(iv) specify the extent to which the process covers entities within the supply chain, including entities upstream in the product supply chain and entities across lines of products or services throughout the covered issuer's product manufacturing.

"(D) The efforts of the covered issuer to ensure that audits of suppliers within the supply chain of the covered issuer are conducted to—

"(i) investigate the working conditions and labor practices of such suppliers;

"(ii) verify whether such suppliers have in place appropriate systems to identify risks of forced labor, slavery, human trafficking, and the worst forms of child labor within their own supply chain; and

"(iii) evaluate whether such systems are in compliance with the policies of the covered issuer or efforts in absence of such policies.

"(E) The efforts of the covered issuer to—

"(i) require suppliers in the supply chain to attest that the manufacture of materials incorporated into any product and the recruitment of labor are carried out in compliance with the laws regarding forced labor, slavery, human trafficking, and the worst forms of child labor;

"(ii) maintain internal accountability standards, supply chain management, and procurement systems, and reporting procedures for employees, suppliers, contractors, or other entities within its supply chain failing to meet the covered issuer's standards regarding forced labor, slavery, human trafficking, and the worst forms of child labor, including a description of such standards, systems, and procedures;

"(iii) train the employees and management who have direct responsibility for supply chain management on issues related to forced labor, slavery, human trafficking, and the worst forms of child labor, particularly with respect to mitigating risks within the supply chains of products; and

"(iv) ensure that labor recruitment practices at all suppliers associated with the supply chain comply with the covered issuer's policies or efforts in absence of such policies for eliminating exploitive labor practices that contribute to forced labor, slavery, human trafficking, and the worst forms of child labor, including by complying with audits of labor recruiters and disclosing the results of such audits.

"(F) The efforts of the covered issuer in cases where forced labor, slavery, human trafficking, and the worst forms of child labor have been identified within the supply chain, to ensure that remedial action is provided to those who have identified as victims, including support for programs designed to prevent the recurrence of those events within the industry or sector in which they have been identified.

"(2) REQUIREMENTS FOR AVAILABILITY OF INFORMATION.—

> "(A) DISCLOSURE ON COMPANY WEBSITE.—The regulations promulgated under paragraph
>
>> (1) shall require that the required information be disclosed by the covered issuer on the Internet website of the covered issuer through a conspicuous and easily understandable link to the relevant information that shall be labeled 'Global Supply Chain Transparency'.
>
> "(B) DISCLOSURE ON COMMISSION WEBSITE.— The Commission shall make available to the public in a searchable format on the Commission's website—
>
>> "(i) a list of covered issuers required to disclose any measures taken by the company to identify and address conditions of forced labor, slavery, human trafficking, and the worst forms of child labor within the covered issuer's supply chain, as required by this subsection; and
>
>> "(ii) a compilation of the information submitted under the rules issued under paragraph (1).

"(3) DEFINITIONS.—As used in this subsection—

> "(A) the term 'covered issuer' means an issuer that has annual worldwide global receipts in excess of $100,000,000;
>
> "(B) the terms 'forced labor', 'slavery', and 'human trafficking' mean any labor practice or human trafficking activity in violation of national and international standards, including International Labor Organization

Convention No. 182, the Trafficking Victims Protection Act of 2000 (Public Law 106–386), and acts that would violate the criminal provisions related to slavery and human trafficking under chapter 77 of title 18, United States Code, if they had been committed within the jurisdiction of the United States;

"(C) the term 'remedial action' means the activities or systems that an issuer puts in place to address non-compliance identified through monitoring or verification, and may apply to individuals adversely affected by the non-compliant conduct or address broader systematic processes;

"(D) the term 'supply chain', with respect to a covered issuer disclosing the information required under the regulations promulgated under this section, means all labor recruiters, suppliers of products, component parts of products, and raw materials used by such entity in the manufacturing of such entity's products whether or not such entity has a direct relationship with the supplier; and

"(E) the term 'the worst forms of child labor' means child labor in violation of national and international standards, including International Labor Organization Convention No. 182.."

184. *Jesner v. Arab Bank, PLC*, No. 16-499, 584 U.S. ___ (more) 138 S. Ct. 1386; 200 L. Ed. 2d 612. Legal conclusion was that foreign corporations may not be sued under the Alien Tort Statute.

*Jesner v Arab Bank* was a case before the United States Supreme Court. The main issue was whether the Alien Tort Statute (formerly known as the Judiciary Act of 1789) allows foreign companies to be named as defendants in lawsuits started in the United States. The Alien Tort Statute gives federal courts power and authority over civil suits brought by foreign nationals.

The majority (5-4) ruled that foreign corporations cannot be sued under the Alien Tort Statute therefore chipping away at the legal options and remedies possible under this law to fight injustices by corporations in foreign countries. United States Supreme Court decision available at https://www.supremecourt.gov/opinions/17pdf/16-499_1a7d.pdf

*Kiobel v. Royal Dutch Petroleum Co.*, 569 U.S. 108 (2013), was another case before the United States Supreme Court and it found that Alien Tort Act does not apply extraterritorially. Yet, this case took a surprise turn when the Supreme Court asked for additional briefing after oral argument was set around the new issue of what circumstances would the Alien Tort Statute, 28 U.S.C. § 1350, allows courts to recognize a cause of action or lawsuit for violations of the law of nations that occur in a sovereign = nation or territory outside the United States. The Court found that presumptively the Alien Tort Statute did not allow a cause of action or lawsuit thereby further taking away at the power of the Alien Tort Statute to remedy injustices by foreign corporations (even if foreign corporations engage in illegal activities). United States Supreme Court decision available at https://www.supremecourt.gov/opinions/12pdf/10-1491_l6gn.pdf.

105. Trade Facilitation and Trade Enforcement Act of 2015 also known as Public Law 114–125. Section 910. Elimination of consumptive demand exception to prohibition of importing goods made with convict labor, forced labor, or indentured labor; report. Available at https://congress.gov/114/plaws/publ125/PLAW-114publ125.pdf.

186. United Nations General Assembly Seventy-Third Session. Working Group on the Issue of Human Rights and Transnational Corporations and Other Business Enterprises. July 16, 2018. Available at https://documents-dds-ny.un.org/doc/UNDOC/GEN/N18/224/87/PDF/N1822487.pdf?OpenElement.

187. Id. at. p. 4

188. Id.

189. Id at p. 6.

190. California Senate Bill No 233. Immunity from Arrest. Approved by Governor Gavin Newsom on July 30,2019 and filed with Secretary of State July 30, 2019. Text of bill available at http://leginfo.legislature.ca.gov/faces/billNavClient.xhtml?bill_id=201920200SB233.

CHAPTER THIRTEEN: A GLOBAL CALL TO ACTION

191. The letter was written by Alianza Nacional de Campesinas. Alianza Nacional de Campesinas is the first women's national organization in the U.S. made of current and former farmworker women as well as women who come from farmworker families. The organization's mission is to "unify the struggle to promote farm worker women's leadership in a national movement to create a broader visibility and advocate for changes that ensure their human rights." Their mission statement and more information available at https://www.alianzanacionaldecampesinas.org.

192. There is a 1 in 400 trillion chance of you being born. The meaning behind this statistic is multi-dimensional. It includes the chance of your grandparents meeting one another and having your Mother and Father independently who go on and later meet and give birth to you. The chance of your parents finding and creating you are astronomical given that there are 6 6 billion people in this world and the number of people each person meets throughout their lifetime is incredibly high. Yet, your parents had you and the statistical chance of that happening given the circumstances you were born into is 1 in 400 trillion. This shows that you are no accident. The world created you for a reason. Yet, most people never realize the miracle that is their life or the purpose behind it. This statistic and concept was beautifully discussed at a TEDx San Francisco talk by Mel Robbins called "How to Stop Screwing Yourself Over," The speaker is an Ivy-League educated lawyer and a career and relationship expert. She discusses how this statistic plays into people's everyday lives and how the actions people fail to take when they don't use the Five Second Rule can impact their present and future. TEDTALK available at https://www.youtube.com/watch?v=Lp7E973zozc.

# ACKNOWLEDGMENTS

In many ways, I feel limited by words when writing this acknowledgment. There are so many people I would like to thank. All angels sent to me. Yet my greatest source of light has always been God for instilling qualities that have helped me throughout my lifetime. Life is not easy, yet I've learned that if we use our gifts for a greater purpose, it makes sense of our journey. It makes sense of our pain. I truly believe that has been God's plan all along.

Writing this book has been a very long and difficult journey for me. One that never would have happened without the continuous love, support, and encouragement of my family. To my parents, thank you for a lifetime of wisdom, grace, and love. Words cannot begin to express my depth of gratitude. To my Mother, you have continued to be a light in my life that leads me to a higher path. I could not have asked for a better role model. If I can be half the person you are, I would be incredibly lucky.

To my sister, Mojahn, you may have left this earth many years ago, but your spirit lives on in the people you loved. You will never be forgotten. Your life changed so many. A spirit like yours never truly dies.

To my husband, Jeremy, you have been a blessing from the first day we met. Thank you for listening to me talk about this book endlessly and for your love, support, patience, and encouragement. I am so grateful for you. You have been the best unexpected gift from the universe.

To my brother, Thatcher, thank you for believing in me and for years of emotional support, love, and words of wisdom. It has made all the difference in the world. You are and always will be my best friend.

To Meredith, Madison, Annika, and Tiffany—you have all been a joy! I am grateful for each of you and for all the love and laughter you have brought to my life. To the rest of my extended family—all of you—I love you!

To the U.S. Fulbright Program, thank you for a once-in-a-lifetime opportunity that completely changed the trajectory of my life. The Fulbright Program gave me the financial freedom and chance to study human trafficking on a deeper level, which led to a lifelong purpose greater than I could have ever imagined or hoped for.

I would also like to personally thank the University of British Columbia Interdisciplinary Graduate Program, Gonzaga University School of Law, Northwestern University's Medill School of Journalism, the United Nations Graduate Summer Program in Geneva, Switzerland, and the United Nations Information Centre in Washington, D.C. These institutions all propelled me forward on my journey in discovering the truth about modern-day slavery and the environment.

To the following individuals, thank you for encouraging me when I felt defeated, helping me carve out my own path, and liberating me to chase and discover my own dreams. Each of you has helped me in your own way. Please accept my deepest gratitude.

Jeremy Bartelson, Ruth Esparza, Father Robert Araujo, Ann Murphy, Sandy Kuhlmann, Kayla Baroch, Tiffany Perez, Michael K. Hawes, Michelle Emond, John Beatty, Patsy Fowler, Janice Matautia, Tom Patch, John Hashew, Karen Smyth, James Vache, Sheila Stillian, Maura Flood, Pam Pschirrer, John Maurice, David DeWolf, Susan Harmon, Jill Moore, Jerri Shepard, Jared Levinson, Kathy and Jon Malone, Dorothy Slater, Jacqueline Porter, Lisa Brewer, Hunter Abell, Brooke Workneh, Cara Nord, Dana Ballout, Dee Gregg, Jennifer Bayley, Jesse Brisendine, Saranne Durham, Karin Ohgren, Gaby Solano, Katie Calloway, Martin Swift, Breean Beggs, Mahdis Keshavarz, Mariam Khan, Jane Schilling, Robin Peltier, Betty Craipo, Shannon Bonogofski Holden, and Shruti Sharma.

Also, I have deep gratitude to Steven Pressfield for writing the book *The War of Art*. That book has helped me and countless others fulfill our dreams and find our own voice.

To those who have lived their lives for a purpose much greater than themselves, you have inspired me by example and taught me that in the end our greatest legacy is what we do for others—not what we do for ourselves.

There's an old saying that some people come into our lives for a season, others a reason, and some stay a lifetime. For those who have come into my life for a moment, for a day, for a year, you have all left an impact in ways I cannot begin to explain.

I realized many years ago that human encounters can be life-changing. Each person has a lesson to teach us. Each soul has a story begging to be told. Thank you for sharing your stories. They have forever changed me.

With admiration,

~Shadan Kapri

# ABOUT THE AUTHOR

Shadan Kapri (pronounced Shadawn Capri) was a U.S. Fulbright Scholar on human rights and trafficking. She has spent the last fifteen years studying and researching the problems of social injustice, modern-day slavery, racism, discrimination, and women's rights. She is also the founder of a boutique law firm and consulting practice, Kapri Law & Consulting, to confront issues impacting women and children.

Kapri Law Firm focuses on international human rights, civil rights, and family law. Kapri Consulting promotes the expansion of human rights by offering services to help companies understand and eliminate all forms of slave labor, forced labor, and child labor in their supply chains while promoting workers' rights and environmental protections.

Her passion for human rights and the environment emerged after volunteering for the United Nations in Geneva, Switzerland, and Washington, D.C. while in law school. She went on to earn advanced degrees from Gonzaga University School of Law, University of British Columbia, and Northwestern University in the areas of law, international relations, and journalism.

Shadan began her legal career at the Washington State Court of Appeals, Division III, as a law clerk by assisting in the research and analyses of over a hundred judicial opinions. Afterwards, she became a prosecutor advocating for children and victims of serious crimes. In the Criminal Division, she prosecuted cases on the trial court and appellate level. They ranged from domestic violence to drinking and driving, child abuse and neglect, assault, kidnapping, attempted murder, and first-degree murder. In the Family Law Division, she advocated on behalf of minor children in contempt-of-court, paternity establishment, and modifications of court orders in the best interest of the child. A sample of her cases can be found at www.shadanslegalcases.wordpress.com.

She is also the recipient of the Daily Point of Light Award. The Daily Point of Light was created by former U.S. President George H. W. Bush to nationally recognize individuals and groups who have a deep commitment to public service.

For more information on the Red Movement, please visit Red-Movement.com.

www.ingramcontent.com/pod-product-compliance
Lightning Source LLC
Chambersburg PA
CBHW060017210326

41520CB00009B/916

*9781734644647*